5/11/08

To IRIS

felisidades

En el Dia de las Madre

# MOM

## Becoming the Mother Every Child Needs and Every Husband Desires

HOLLY ANDERSON

Winword
publishing house
Phoenix, Arizona

FIRST EDITION

Published by **Winword Publishing House**
3520 E. Brown Road
Mesa, AZ 85213
480-985-6156

ISBN 13 978-1-58588-026-3

*MOM, Becoming the Mother Every Child Needs and Every Husband Desires*

**Printed in Canada**

To order or for more information, contact us at:

480-985-6156

or visit: www.DadMomBook.com

MOM

## Table of Contents


Dedication 1

Introduction 5

1 I Refuse to Ask For Directions 9

2 The Book Is 'Finished,' and 'It Is Good!' 23

3 Mom, Are You Sure This Bridge Will Hold Me? 43

4 It's Time You Put Your Husband in His Place 57

5 Eight Ways to Meet Your Husband's Needs: Sex, Sex, Sex, Sex, Sex, Sex, Food and Sleep 77

6 Living a Life Of No Regrets 105

7 Creating Memories 123

8 Liar Liar! 139

9 I'm Sorry—What Did You Say? 153

10 I Still Can't Hear You 167

11 No Chapter 11 In Honor of Baylor

12 It Wouldn't Be an Argument If You'd Just Let Me Be Right 189

13 Your Child's Secret Place 205

14 Being the Source of Encouragement in Your House 217

15 Give Me a Hug 243

16 I Will Be Going to School With You Today 249

17 I Love You! Now Leave Me Alone 261


MOM

# MOM

MOM

## Dedication

I dedicate this book, first and foremost, to God. Without His grace, strength, and wisdom, I would not have attempted to write this book. Thank You, Lord, for always being there and for giving me nothing but the best in my life.

I also dedicate this book to my very best friend and the man who swept me off my feet. Scot, you are everything I always knew I always wanted, and without you, my life would be void of so much that is good. You've been my source of encouragement; that person bold enough to love me, support me, laugh with me, argue with me, vacation with me, stand up for me and parent with me. You are the reason I've become the person I am today. You always push me to the next level; have stood beside me, cheering for me and believing in me. God must really love me a lot; because He gave me you! Thank you for being the man that you are; the man who strives to be a better person every day! Thank you for being motivated and self-confident, for persevering and loving me in the midst of my ugly and unlovable moments and for always considering me. Thank you for being the most amazing dad any little boy or little girl could ever pray for. Your passion and love for your children are immeasurable. I am extremely blessed to be your wife and desire to show you just how much I love you for the rest of our days. Thank you for being awesome you!

I need to take some time to let the "other men" in my life know the impact they have made in me. Laken, Heath, Baylor, and Peyton: I could never express in words how you have changed my life. Ever since I can remember, I have wanted to be a mom. But, nothing could have ever prepared me for the love I feel in having been given you. You make me proud and strong. In your presence I can do and accomplish anything. I love each one of you, and am amazed with every passing day; that you kind hearted, compassionate, intelligent, witty and talented young men are mine. You are, undoubtedly, the greatest achievements of my life. I love you.

I would also like to dedicate this book to my parents—I appreciate all your training, support, encouragement, love, understanding and prayers through my journey of becoming me. I have within me characteristics that were placed there by you. I thank you for directing me to be a strong, confident, compassionate, other-minded, loving, self-controlled, intelligent, educated and spiritual person. I've watched you persevere through tough times and come out the winner. I watched as you laid down your lives for other people's children, for no other reason than to show them they were not forgotten, but greatly loved. I am forever grateful that you challenged me to be happy and ever optimistic regardless of what life would try to throw me. I love you and give you the credit you deserve and earned.

To Kimberly and Ryan, I am so proud to be your big sister. It has been my extreme pleasure to have grown up alongside both of you, while "bossing" you around. In many ways, you were the beginning of my motherhood training. All too often mom would have to say, "Holly, I'm the mom, thank you." I have so many fond memories of growing up together, and I just want each of you to know how incredibly proud I am of who you are today. We had a very different childhood, and we, as most families, have been through our share of hard times. But, I have watched you persevere, reaching and accomplishing what you have desired. You are amazing examples of what a person can achieve with positive thinking, humor, compassion and determination. "I already have plans for my biscuit, and they involve butter!"

I can't write a book on being a mom without thanking my closest friends who are also moms and M.O.D. You have no idea the support you give me in our joint destinies of becoming awesome moms. I appreciate you listening, praying, understanding and being bold enough to share your less than stellar mom moments! A person can't do this thing called "motherhood" alone, or in the absence of people who understand and can "relate." I'm inspired, in awe, and encouraged by all of you. Not one of you will have fallen short on this quest to be "one of the best." I know that at the end of your lives, your children will call you their "best friend and Hero!"

Thank you to the publishers and editors on this book. Everyone should know that it is you who make this idea become a reality. I appreciate you making it the best it can possibly be. I want to also thank the proofing team. I'm sure making this grammatically correct and cohesive was a huge undertaking! Thanks to Dave for pushing this and connecting with the "powers that be." Derek, what can I say? You are soo superbly "graphic" and good at it too! Lastly, I thank my in-laws and pastors for their continued support of our endeavors, their insight, wisdom and prayers, but mostly for giving me: Scot, the man I will forever love and parent with.

## INTRODUCTION

When reading this book, please understand that we all make mistakes—even we moms! (I know it's hard to believe, and IF we have, they've been few).

We all have made mistakes and will undoubtedly make some more in the future. But, this is where the beauty begins, because being an awesome mom isn't about the absence of mistakes. Being a great mom is about learning from the ones we've made so as not to repeat them again. Our mistakes give us knowledge that enables us to move forward in our quest and to do so successfully. Being an awesome mom isn't about our lack of character or integrity exhibited during those moments of extreme exhaustion and adult temper tantrums. It is our overall character, our extreme passion, dedication, commitment and love that we demonstrate to our kids throughout each day and throughout our lives that matters and counts the most!

My mom, after whom I try to pattern my life, could have messed up a lot when I was a child. I'm sure that she has her share of regrets and "if onlys." But, if she did, I don't remember it, because all the good, all the things that she did right, far outweighed any negative. I can't recall or make you a list of her bad choices or decisions, because there was too much good in our lives.

Also, realize that great moms are not born; they are developed. Every mom has inside her the potential to be the awesome mom she desires to be. But, like anything in life, it takes understanding to reach our goals. We must first find out the "how" to being an awesome mom, then choose to make any necessary changes to implement that "how," and finally, add a lot of practice and continuously exercise the "how." Being a great mom isn't something you just try or even do for eighteen years. It becomes something you do and live for the rest of your life because your being great comes from the inside—from the heart. You have to dedicate yourself to never stop growing, to never stop changing, regardless of how painful it may be to change, and to always pursue being the best mom you can be.

I write this book, not from my experience of being a great mom, but from my experience of being a daughter of a great mom. That's a different twist. You see, I can't write this book on the premise that I have "arrived." I can't say, "Look at me. I've done it. I was a great mom. I raised my nine-year-old to perfection. He doesn't do drugs, hardly ever cusses, and we just got him off cigarettes (that is a joke)."

I can't say, "Look at what I have done." But I can say, "Look at what my mom accomplished." And I can share with you what I experienced as a daughter—how my mom made me feel and what was developed in me because of my relationship with her. It's a whole new perspective on being a mom, an outlook worthy of being explored.

So this isn't a book written by a mom who has no relationship with her kids. It's written by a daughter whose mom can be called a hero and best friend. I am writing this as a daughter who desires that same kind of relationship with my own children. I thank God for my mom, and I work hard at becoming as good a mom as she is today.

I believe if you and I do everything in this book, one day your kids, too, will be saying, "My mom is my hero and my best friend."

MOM

# Chapter 1

## I Refuse to Ask for Directions

*When a mom has no vision, the relationship she desires with her family perishes...*

Imagine with me, if you will, your vacation that you have spent 351 days, 50 long weeks, over 5,000 mom hours earning. You have wiped and changed over 1,200 dirty butts, picked up over 2,500 socks, said the phrase "I'm not your maid" well over 1,000 times, flipped the toilet lid down 972 times (the exact number of times you went to the bathroom), answered the phrase, "Mom (or Honey), where is my…," 12,362 times, said "Honey, I have a headache," 365 times (actually only 3 times, the other 362 times you thought it, but decided to just keep it to yourself). This is your vacation.

Vacation for you starts three days before the actual date—for the responsibility of packing the entire family is, has and always will be the responsibility of the mom. Every woman and man knows that when mom is not in charge of the packing, someone will go without underwear, a toothbrush, the favorite "blankie," shoes, belts, deodorant, snow jacket, map… you get the picture. This task means washing every piece of laundry in the house, (which the husband feels should be able to be accomplished in an hour or two). You must wash, fold, and then plan out what each member of the family will be wearing for the next two weeks. I also need to pack all toiletries, medication, snacks, games, entertainment, DVDs, beach supplies, towels, diapers, wipes, bottles, formula, baby food, baby cups, baby plates, baby toys, baby blankets, baby crib, baby sheets, baby pillow. I need all the kids' books, homework, their toys, Game Boys, Game Boy games… (You so know the list).

Sometimes I wonder if hell is an eternity in which all the women do is pack the luggage for all the men going to heaven. While you spend fifteen hours a day doing this, your husband must conserve and build up his energy needed for vacation by participating in a ritual, otherwise known to many scientists as "watching television." While he is getting ready, he so blesses you with tidbits of much appreciated and needed information like, "Don't forget to pack my underwear!" and, "Don't forget to pack that shirt I like, the red one" (you mean the one that I couldn't stand, and would pack if I hadn't thrown it away three years ago!). Something in you wants him to pay, just a little. So you under pack him to teach him a small but very rewarding lesson. You pack him three pairs of underwear for the fourteen-day trip. But this always backfires in that he never complains, which presents a whole new area of concern for proper hygiene or lack of.

You work until three o'clock in the morning the night before because for reasons known only by men, your husband's biggest concern in life right now is making better time than any other man he knows. He has to leave by 5:00 a.m. sharp to beat traffic. For the next three weeks, this incredible feat of prowess will be the topic of conversation with every person he meets. "Yep. I made the trip in three hours and nineteen minutes. I cut three minutes off the trip by lightening the overall vehicle weight by not wearing a belt, shoes or underwear." Again, the scary proper hygiene thing.

From 4:00 a.m. until we leave at noon, all I hear about is how I over packed. All the while I'm thinking, "I'm sure those three days of TV time gave you the energy and the mental capacity to figure it out!"

As I load the children into the car, I notice that the inside of our vehicle looks like one of those baggage trams at the airport. There really is no organization to the madness at all. "Honey, did you pack the car blindfolded this year to add a level of difficulty?" Bags are thrown and strewn all over. He literally has my two-year-old sitting on a suitcase and two duffel bags. He is trying to convince my son that they are a couple of nice pillows and that the higher seating

Sometimes I wonder if hell is an eternity in which all the women do is pack the luggage for all the men going to heaven.

elevation makes video viewing better. My husband explains to me that we need to pull out a bunch of luggage, then load the kids, then put the luggage back in place. I chuckle, thinking about the fact that we will be stopping for lunch and he will have to repeat this process several times over. He then explains that the luggage adds a level of safety that airbags could never give us. I say, "You load them up. I will be back."

I come back and my husband says we are ready; kids and luggage are loaded up. I have to take his word for it because I can't see a single child. As I'm getting in, my husband (the love of my life) continues to complain about all the stuff I packed. I can only respond with, "Yes, Sweetie, next year I will start packing weeks earlier. I can only imagine how frustrated those two long hard hours of packing the car have made you."

He keeps going on and on and on and on about all the luggage. Once again it is lesson time in the Anderson home. Scot must be taught a lesson, not so much for him, but for my personal pleasure. As soon as he is in the car, seatbelt on, maps out, has put the car in reverse, I say, "Honey, I forgot a bag. Can you go get it for me?" (Now, that is funny, because every bag we own is in this vehicle!).

He looks like a wounded bear. I can tell he is going to snap, but I know from fifteen years of marriage how far I can push until he does. So I suppress my tiny feelings of guilt. Today I will be taking you right to the edge. Enjoy the ride, my love. He slams the vehicle into park, and quite honorably restrained says, “Where is this stupid bag?”

I had to think fast. Finally I said, “It is my scrap book bag!”

He comes back, wedges the bag under my three-year-old, convincing him that it’s another pillow. Then backing out of the driveway, luggage, kids, and scrap-book bag in tow, I hear my son say, “Dad! I have to go…” (You fill in the blank, but I can guarantee you know the answer.)

He places the car in park and makes the official bathroom announcement to all: “IF YOU HAVE TO GO TO THE BATHROOM, GO NOW! I WILL NOT BE STOPPING FOR ANOTHER FIVE HUNDRED MILES!” He unloads all the luggage, gets the children out. They go to the bathroom, come back, load up again. A little dance is being done in my very soul at this moment. So shameful.

Seven minutes into our long-awaited journey, a small scuffle breaks out in the back seat over which video we will be playing first. Don’t we all just LOVE the concept of TV in the car? I mean, as if I don’t already play referee enough as it is.

At this point, I can tell my love has reached his limit. I have taken him too far, and now I need to do some damage control. Too late! Like a madman, he whips the car across three lanes of traffic to the bicycle lane. He stops the car and makes the official "let-the-vacation-begin" announcement: "IF I HEAR ONE MORE PEEP OUT OF ANYONE, I WILL TURN THIS CAR AROUND AND GO HOME!"

This is where I so gently and lovingly lean over, give him a kiss on the cheek, and with a sense of gentle curiosity in my voice, say, "So what got you in such a bad mood?"

If you're a mom, I know you can relate to my account of the rigors of taking a family trip! But now imagine with me that, after all of this, you begin your vacation only to realize you have indeed forgotten to plan the one thing necessary for a successful trip: your destination.

"Where are you going?" someone asks.

And you have to reply, "I don't know."

Think about it. Without an intended destination, how do you know if you're going in the right direction? And how do you know when you've arrived?

Of course, you understand that you can't begin a trip without a destination, without having some goal or vision, if you will, as to where you will end up. Without a vision, you will never arrive! And you will have no idea as to how to prepare.

**A Vision for Motherhood**

It is the same with being a mom. Many moms leave on the "trip" of mothering (and it is a trip!) without having any idea where they're going. They have no real vision for being a mom. Sure, they want their kids to grow up well and be successful but just having that as a goal is as vague as my saying, "I want to go somewhere warm and sunny on my vacation!"

Think about this. What you pack and how you prepare for your vacation depends on where you're going. All of your planning, including the maps you'll take, the amount of money you'll need, and so forth, depends on your intended destination. You can't get there if you don't know where there is.

You can't get there if you don't know where there is.

In much the same way, many moms get excited about the new baby, and they jump in the car of life, speeding ahead toward what they think is the land of great mothering. The problem is, they don't know where "it" is. So they find themselves backtracking and feeling frustrated until they finally give up on their desire to be a great mom and settle for just being a mom.

The simple truth of the matter is this: Without vision, you will not be able to be an awesome mom.

Nearly every book on leadership or success stresses the importance of having a vision for whatever it is you are planning on doing. I read a great book once that said, "Where there is no vision, the people perish..." Dreams, aspirations, and the desires of your heart, including your desire to be a great mom, perish without vision. Another translation: "Where there is no vision, the people are unrestrained."

Vision brings parameters, borders and boundaries into your life. With vision, you have controls that keep you moving toward the fulfillment of your vision. That vision guards and protects your desire because it brings restraint into your life that won't allow you to do anything that would interfere with that desire coming to pass.

The opposite of that is true, too. When you lack vision, you lack the controls or restraints you need to move you toward your desire. You have no parameters in place to protect what it is you desire to accomplish or do.

For example, most of us can remember a time when we really wanted something in life. Maybe it was a special dress, shoes, Barbie's playhouse, or even a car or house. Up until the time of that desire, perhaps we couldn't save a dime. We had no restraints in our lives where saving money was concerned. But then we got a vision. A mighty motivator! That vision would not allow us to waste our money. That vision may have caused us to work extra hours or take on another job. Our vision had so much power that it drove us toward the desire of our hearts and would not let up until we had whatever it was we wanted.

Vision is one of the most powerful forces given to us. People often confuse vision with desire, but the two are distinctly different.

Desire is simply something you want. Vision is something you will have.

Desire is something you need. Vision is something you can't live without.

Desire will give you something to think about. Vision will give you something to live for! Vision will instill passion!

A vision for being an awesome mom won't allow you to invest your time in things that will take time away from your children. For example, you may want to spend another night on the phone with the friend that has had the same problems for the last five years. But when you get a vision for great mothering, that vision will not allow you to do that. Your vision will push you toward putting forth the effort and hard work it takes to be a great mom. Your vision will not allow you to put others' needs before your children's needs. It will not permit you to make empty promises. It will not allow you to stop growing and changing as a mom. It will continually push you toward being the mom you desire and deserve to be.

Ladies, don't let this next paragraph make you mad. Let's be honest here. We all know this is true. Let's apply vision to women and weight loss. Let's say that a wife is struggling with her weight. She wants to lose weight, but she just can't seem to do it. Her metabolism or her genetic makeup just won't allow it!

Now, I'm not perfect, but maybe it is the buttered popcorn, nachos, and candy we had to have at the movies. Or maybe it's all the fast-food meals we super-size that have caused us to be super-sized! Or, could it be the many trips to Starbucks in which we choose the highest caloric drink they serve—twice!

Then suppose the marriage, for whatever reason, goes to divorce court. In seemingly no time at all, just in a couple of months, she drops thirty or forty pounds and is looking good!

What happened? Did her metabolism miraculously change? Did the divorce papers change her DNA? No, of course not. She went past desire and got to vision. She sees that she wants to be married, maybe find another husband, maybe desires for her ex-husband to want her back, or just wanted to prove something to herself. To do that, she lost the weight. The vision to lose weight was "birthed" inside of her, and that vision brought restraints into her life. She began refusing junk food, making healthy choices instead. She began working out consistently. Those options were always available to her; she just didn't know how to tap into the power of vision.

Now let's apply the same truth to kids. If you place vision in their hearts for something worthwhile, you will watch them head toward success, fulfilling their dreams and goals.

We can also see the power of vision in kids keeping themselves sexually pure. Just telling kids that premarital sex is bad will not keep them from being promiscuous. If anything, it will make it even more appealing. But what if you put a vision for abstinence into their hearts?

~

She went past desire and got vision.

~

For example, share with your children that losing their virginity steals from the one they will marry one day. Explain to them the risks and the rewards. (If you don't know the rewards, read some books on it.) Put in their hearts the great things they can expect when they follow the road less traveled. Then they will have the restraints in their lives that will not allow them to be with someone who is all wrong for them, someone who doesn't share their vision. Their vision will protect their desire.

If you put a vision within your children for hanging out with the right crowd, doing well in school, getting a college degree or some form of higher education, you will train them up in the way they should go, and that vision will steady and restrain them along life's path and not allow them to depart from it. Sure, they may find and experience their own rough patches along the way, but vision assists in helping them get back on track.

Real vision always brings parameters into your life that will guide you toward the fulfillment of your desire. You can't just have a desire for a certain outcome—even a strong desire. You have to have the vision for it, which brings with it the determination that you will have it.

Let's take this idea of vision a step further. Suppose you want to quit smoking. You desire it. You've set seemingly thousands of goals and have thrown your cigarettes away hundreds of times. You've thrown your smokes on the altar and then went home mad because you wasted three bucks worth of cigarettes! You see, desires alone are not strong enough to overcome the flesh. You need the power of vision. For some people, that vision will come when the doctor says, "If you don't quit smoking, you'll be dead in a year." Suddenly, vision is birthed, and they are now able to quit. That vision won't allow them to smoke. It is more powerful than their desire.

Do you know why extramarital affairs happen? A lack of vision. Where there is no vision, marriages perish. But vision will not allow you to have an affair. It doesn't matter how much your human nature wants to do it—vision will not allow it. Vision protects your desire to have a great marriage, a marriage that's "heaven on earth." That vision is stronger than any physical desire. It won't matter that another man is attractive—your vision is more desirable! The pull may be strong, but the vision is stronger.

You see, a desire is something you hope for, but a vision is something you obtain. A desire only gives you thoughts of success, but a vision actually brings you toward that success. If you want to receive and enjoy the desires of your heart, you need vision. Vision will produce your desires.

This should excite you! Every one of us has desires, things we want in our lives. How do we get them? Vision. We want to be great moms. How do we get there? Vision. We have to learn how to tap into the power of vision—seeing ourselves where we want to be!

# Chapter 2

## This Book Is 'Finished,' and 'It Is Good!'

*...Write the vision, and make it plain upon tables, that he may run that readeth it.*

This is my husbands story, but it is one of my favorites. Sit back and read his story, as you get a glimpse into the world I get to enjoy every day of our awesome marriage.

Scot writes: "Last January I had surgery on my right knee. After six months of rehab and exercise, I was going to have a strength test performed on the knee. At that point, I was excited, because if I passed this strength test and my right leg was as strong as my left leg, I could play sports again.

"So I drive all the way out to Phoenix to this huge gym, where the strength test will be performed. I walk in the door and it is an amazing sight, because—and, please, don't tell my wife—as far as the eye could see, there are beautiful women. It's like the training center for a college girls' volleyball team. (Correction: I am only assuming they were beautiful, because I am married and did not look.)

"Finally, I see the only guy in this gym, and he's behind the desk. He's a surfer guy. I didn't know these guys still existed, but there he is. He's unshaven and has the long curly hair, the OP tank top, and the surfer shorts. I walk up to him, and he says, 'What's up, D..u..d..e?' with that long drawn-out surfer d…u…d…e.

"I answer, 'I'm here for my knee, (slight unsure pause) Dude.'

"Then he says, 'Cool, D..u..d..e. You, like, need to fill out some paperwork.'

"I say, 'Cool, Dude.'

"So I take the paperwork, fill it out, and give it back to 'Spicoli.' He then brings out this very pretty lady (I assume she was pretty—didn't look). Michelle is going to do my training with me.

"Now, realize that I have not done any exercise in a year except to go upstairs and go to bed. That has been the extent of my daily exercise program.

"Michelle, 'Little Miss Jane Fonda,' decides to get me going on a 'marathon.' She puts the incline on the treadmill as high as it will go and gets me running, and running, and running. Finally, just before I was going to pass out, she says, 'Good. We're done running.'

"Oh thank sweet Jesus, I think. Then she hands me a rope and says, 'Let's jump.' Then after what seems to be an eternity, she says, 'Now let's jump from side to side; now let's jump high; now let's double jump…' Then, 'Run in place.' And after that, 'Climb these steps one jillion times.'

"I don't exactly remember what happened next, but I think I began to cry like a little girl. I began to pray that Jesus would just take me right then. I'm crying out similar to how I picture Moses screaming out to Pharaoh, 'LET MY PEOPLE GO!!!' I feel like I have endured all the plagues, and it is time to set me free.

I don't exactly remember what happened next, but I think I began to cry like a little girl.

"Now that I can't move my leg, I am informed that we're ready to do the strength test.

"Now remember, I want my right knee to be as strong as the left knee. If it is, I can play sports again. As we're doing the stretches and the leg curls, my knee is doing great. Finally, we get to the leg press. I push up 240 pounds three times with my left leg. Little Miss Fonda says, 'Okay, now the right leg.'

"Please picture the scene with me. To my right are four pretty girls doing sit-ups (or something like that, because I didn't look). Then over to my left are a couple of girls passing a medicine ball back and forth. In front of me, there is a group of girls doing leg-extension exercises. And my training lady is right beside me. So within three feet of my world are about ten women. With everything in my very being, I begin pushing with the right leg. I want it to be strong, so I'm giving it everything I've got. Each time I push, I keep arching my back, and Little Jane keeps saying, 'Stop arching your back. Let's try that again.'

"So here we go. I'm pushing with everything I've got, and I'm halfway there. I feel like the veins in my neck are going to burst. She cries out, 'Stop arching your back!' And then she pushes on my stomach.

"Now, you know, of course, that you don't ever, ever, ever push on a man's stomach while he is pushing anything, because if you do, he'll lose all control over what his body will do afterward. (They should teach women that in physical therapy school, don't you think? It should be Lesson 28 or something: 'Don't push on a man's belly. If you do, this is what's going to happen, and it will make this kind of mess.')

"So Jane pushes, and a noise sounds forth from my backside that could be heard for a city block: FHPPPHGURGLEFHPPHGURGLEFHPPPHTH. It was the single worst fart I have ever passed in my life. There has been some fierce competition, but that one was the worst.

"Little Jane's eyes looked like they were going to pop out. Her mouth dropped, and I was speechless, afraid that I had blown the seat apart behind me. I turned to see if I had shot my spleen out somewhere. I think we were all surprised that the fire sprinklers didn't go off.

"Everything in the gym stops. About forty girls stop what they're doing and look over at me. And why wouldn't they? They probably thought some terrorist act had occurred.

"Time freezes. I'm just sitting there. In my mind, my life flashes before my eyes. I begin to ask God what to do. I think, Your Word has no instructions about this. Your Word is supposed to be for every circumstance, but there's nothing in there for this. I feel like You lied to me. A thought pops into my head that says, 'Run, Man. Just run and never look back.' But I can't run; my legs are too tired. Then a beautiful thought comes to mind: Blame it on Jane Fonda. That worked in junior high.

"Just as I was about to say to her, 'You're disgusting!' it was like God stepped in and answered my prayers. Everyone went back to doing what they were doing—like nothing even happened. Sure they'll all laugh later, I thought, but we're adults here. Let's just ignore it.

"But just then, from across the room, Surfer Boy cries out, 'D..U..D..E! I heard that all the way over here, D.u.d.e!'

"Laughter erupts such as the earth has never heard. Grown women are rolling on the floor laughing so hard they can't breathe. My trainer drops to her knees and starts laughing uncontrollably.

"For the remainder of the session, every time I walk by Surfer Boy, he has a funny little comment for me, like, 'Bro—you smell like corn nuts, Dude!'"

It's funny things like this that happen to us in life that show us what things are important in the grand scheme and what are not. Being embarrassed in front of a small army of Wonder Women is not very important, relatively speaking. Being a great mom to my kids and having them be a part of my life until I pass from this life is very, very important.

To achieve this goal of being world's awesome mom takes more than six months of intensive training and exercise. It takes a lifestyle of building relationships. Where do we begin? The obvious answer is from the moment your kids are born. But assuming you haven't always done the right thing because you haven't known what to do, we'll start with your vision for being a great mom.

**'Finishing' Before You Start**

An important part in having a vision for being a great mom is writing down your vision and making it plain. But a key part of writing a vision is finishing it before you start it, that is, "seeing" it, or "visualizing" it in its finished state. For example, when you're planning a vacation, you "finish" the vacation before you start it.

You plan where you'll be going, how long you'll be gone, where you'll stay, what you need to pack, how much money you'll need, and so forth. Once it is finished, then you start it.

Similarly, to be a great mom, you have to finish being a great mom (see it in your mind) so you can start being a great mom.

If you and I are going to have a vision, we must develop this skill of "finishing before we start"—this ability to "see" it before it happens. We already do this in various ways every day. For example, we see dinner done before we cook it. We see our house built before the contractors start building it.

> If you and I are going to have a vision, we must develop this skill of "finishing before we start."

To build a house, you don't just start throwing walls up. You have to have detailed plans written down. You have to have a plan as to where every wire and outlet will be placed, where all the pipes will be installed, and so forth. You picture where the kids will sleep, and decide whether you will have individual formal living and dining rooms as well as a family room. Once you have all the plans, the house is "finished." Then you start to build it. If you start building it before your plans are finished, the outcome could be disastrous. For example, you might pour concrete and then realize you need plumbing. So you have to tear up the concrete, put in the plumbing, and redo the concrete. Then, oops, you forgot the plumbing for yet another bathroom, so you tear it up one more time. Or, maybe you were considering placing the laundry room upstairs nearer to the bedrooms, but hadn't shared that with your spouse, thus there is no plumbing near to support even the suggestion of that idea.

Without written plans, you would be constantly tearing up what you've already done in order to fix problems. This describes life for some people. They start something—in the way of disciplining their children, for example—and then, oops, they forgot something, and they have to start all over. They have to rethink the whole thing. They'll say, "Well, that doesn't work. Let's try this." Then if that doesn't work, they try this and this and this. Had they "finished" it before they started it, they wouldn't have had to keep going back and starting over.

If you don't finish your vision—if you don't know where you're going—you're going to be constantly backtracking, throwing away what you've been working on, and the time it took right alongside with it.

"What if I finish it wrong?" someone asked.

Let's say that you're on your way to San Diego, and there is a detour that you didn't know about. Your directions showed no indication of a detour. Does that mean that it is futile to write directions and plot your course?

No, of course not! Under that type of thinking, you would never write down directions because there might be a detour along the way. But you would be planning for failure if you did that. No, you finish your trip, then you start your trip. And if there happens to be an unexpected detour, you flow with it.

Things will change in life, but you have to have a vision and then just flow with the change. Concerning motherhood, you have to finish it, start it, and be able to flow with change if it comes. In other words, it is important that your vision remains finished but that you be flexible.

I've heard it said, "It is impossible to steer a bicycle that isn't moving." How true that is concerning our lives. It is impossible to get anywhere if you don't start moving.

So, together, let's "finish" our children right now, so we can start our journey to being great moms.

In a sense, I am finishing this book in this one chapter. I am setting forth and finishing the vision on which the rest of the chapters will be built. Once I finish this, I can write the rest. In this chapter, I will show you my vision for being an awesome mom. As you read it, feel free to take with you those things you want to see at the end of your own journey.

First, the obvious things I want my children to have are good habits. Now, we tend to think of a habit in terms of a bad habit, something we want to quit doing but we can develop good habits, too. In fact, I believe that habits are something given to us to help in our success. If I train certain habits into the hearts of my children, when they get old, they will not break those habits.

For example, my children will have a habit of growing, changing, and becoming better in life. They will grow to be adults who strive to be a better spouse, better in their profession, better in life. These things become habits. Then, even though they might want to just stay the same, they can't, because this habit will be hard to break.

I also want my children to have a habit of loving others. They may want to be mean or not want to love. But they can't, because of this habit of loving others that's inside them. Then one day, when marriage gets a little tough and those around them say, "Just give up," they won't, because they'll have the habit of love and dedication. That habit will push them toward attending marriage seminars and reading books on the subject of marriage. That habit will eventually drive them into having an amazing marriage. They will have developed a habit of not simply pointing the finger at someone else, but accepting responsibility and accountability for how they contribute to change.

My children will also have a habit of not giving up. When others have quit and walked away from their dreams, my children will have a habit of persevering, of giving their all. This habit will lead them into a habit of success. Even if they wanted to be unsuccessful, they couldn't, because of this unbreakable habit of persevering.

They will have a habit of being happy. They may want to join the other eighty percent of the world that can find unhappiness in anything, but they will choose to look at the good things in life. They will see problems as nothing more than opportunities to grow and change—as challenges to be conquered. They will see every day as a great day. They will expect the best out of life. The interesting thing is, whatever you expect you almost always get.

So my first vision for my children is good habits. My second vision is at the heart of this book. It is one of my greatest desires for them now, and for when they grow up, to be able to say that they have and know with me what my mom and I have today—friendship.

> My children will also have a habit of not giving up.

**The Heart of the Vision**

My mom and I have a great friendship and relationship. To me, my relationship with my kids is vitally important, too. I don't want them to grow up, move away, call me on the holidays, and see me twice a year. I don't want the majority of their remembrances to be of me barking out orders or of my constant struggle to get them to remember to brush their teeth and make their beds. Of course, I want my kids to be successful in all that they do, but I also want them to be my best friends, just as I consider my mom to be mine.

I want my kids to look forward to spending time with me. I want time with mom to be something they are excited about doing, not something they have to do. I want them to honor me because they want to, not because they have to. I want them to love talking to me because of what we have together as friends—not feel as though they have to talk to me in order to bypass a heaping load of guilt and nagging! I've heard many moms say, "I hope I don't turn out like my mom." I work hard at trying to become just like mine. I want my children to say the same thing about me.

Notice how I'm setting a much different goal for mothering than society has often set. I say that being a great mom is about developing a relationship with my children. Society has more than once implied that being a great mom is to provide a loving home. Society's goal has a different destination than mine. On my way to relationship, I will certainly pass through providing a loving home for my children, but my destination will be vastly different. My vision goes way beyond society's vision for great mothering.

At the end of life, doesn't society judge moms largely on how well they created a loving home? People will say, "She was a great mom. She always put food on the table, and love in the air." Nobody mentions that she perhaps hadn't talked to her children in ten years and some of them didn't even go to the funeral! But in society's eyes, she was considered a great mom. Many would say, "The kids were just spoiled." But, listen, things only spoil when they're put in the wrong environment. If the kids are spoiled, somewhere along the way mom failed, too.

I believe that a mom who provided a loving home for her children fulfilled a role of a mom, all right, but she fell way short of being a great mom! She failed to nurture and develop a relationship with them. The things she provided for her kids could not take the place of having a relationship with them.

In this book, I'm saying that there is a higher level of mothering that is based on the relationship between mom and child. This relationship is the vision, the "finished product" that a great mom strives to see fulfilled.

As I said, society says that a mom must provide a loving home to be a great mom. I am not discounting the providing of that loving environment. That's good and highly important, but I want more. I want to go beyond the norm. I want my children still coming to me for advice and still wanting to spend time with me when they are in their twenties and older. I want to have a great relationship with all of my children, a relationship that just keeps getting better our whole lives. And one day, when I'm 120 and I pass from this earth, my children will say, "There lies my mom and my best friend. We shared many years of great memories together!"

Can you see how a vision is finished now? With that in mind, can you see how that changes what you do as a mom today? Do you see the power of vision? Your vision for being a great mom will change who you are and who you become to your children. It will change the time you spend with them, but more importantly, it will change the kind of time you spend with them. And change what that time spent produces in their and your lives!

**The Focus of Our Vision: Spending Time or Building Relationships?**

I'm sure we all have heard the terms "quality time" and "quantity time," and we've heard it said, "It's not the quantity of time you spend with your children, but the quality of time you spend with them." More often than not, this is quoted as an excuse a mom uses to soothe her conscience. Moms will spend seven hours of quantity time with the phone and household chores, and then thirty minutes of so-called quality time with their kids. "But it was quality time," they'll say. Really? What made it quality time?

When you talk about quantity of time and quality of time, what is the focus? Time! Both are time-centered. If your vision is to spend quality time with your children, you have a vision, or destination, that is focused on time rather than on relationship. Time becomes the priority; time is first, relationship-building is second. In other words, your children's needs are bound to time rather than your time being bound to their needs!

Spending quality and quantity time with our children is very important. We need to do that. But if you're using time to determine whether you're a good mom or not, at the end of life, you will come up short of your vision of having a close friendship with your kids.

Many moms who have no relationship with their children today played with their kids, had tea parties with their daughters, took their kids to the park. They would say that they did do things with their children just like other moms. Those are great activities, but the moms who did these things and didn't build a relationship during the activity simply wasted time. Sure, the kids got to run around, maybe get some exercise, maybe strengthen sibling relationships, but what did it add to the mom/child relationship? Without a specific focus on relationship building amidst time spent together, the relationship doesn't really grow.

The moms who did these things and didn't build a relationship during the activity simply wasted time.

I want to touch on something here that we will discuss in depth in chapters yet to come. It's the concept of balance. I understand that as moms we get busy, and have much on our plate by way of deadlines and time constraints. I understand that there will be times when we are with our children, but our thoughts are elsewhere and the kids are fine, times where we are simply observers. I realize that it's unrealistic to think that every amount of our time spent with our kids will be about building an amazing relationship, but what are you characterized by? It is going to be imperative that we adopt a healthy understanding and usage of balance, the knowing of when we have and haven't made relationship a focus. My intention is not to diminish the sweetness and need of quiet times simply spent in one another's company, watching in awe and wonder, but rather to make sure we give each their due worth and value.

Sometimes moms, out of their desire to get ahead of or stay on top of the never ending, ever growing pile of laundry, beds to make, chore charts to manage, sport practices, dental visits, homework papers, baths, mealtimes, spend more time thinking of ways to organize the chaos, than actually organizing the chaos so they free up time, time that can be used in the building of their relationship with their children. Many moms think that having the kids with them during errands qualifies as time spent together. Sure, the kids may be in the vehicle with you, but is the relationship benefiting from this time spent with one another? Or, are they watching a movie while you process all the other routes you need to navigate in order to get dinner on the table by five? This taxi ride is a perfect opportunity to talk and encourage your children to share. You may be spending time with them, but is the time being used to better the relationship?

Do you see how time can become the goal instead of relationship? There are a lot of moms and children out there who merely tolerate each other, but who spent time together as the children were growing up. My mom told me some time ago not to grade myself as a mom on the quality and quantity of time I spend with my children, but on the quality and quantity of the relationship that comes out of the time I spend with him or her.

Time is important but it's not our goal. When having a relationship with your kids is your goal, it will change how you spend your time with them. I recently grasped this point in my own personal life.

Three of our four sons take piano lessons, and they each are to practice twenty to thirty minutes a day. This wasn't getting accomplished on its own, so I set up specific times where I could sit and make sure that they practiced and assist if they needed it. But, all the other things that needed me would gnaw inside my mind, and I would get agitated that they were not able to govern this time for themselves; that I had to sit like a jailer while a million other tasks were set aside. Within minutes I would be at full boil, and the merest hint of needing help would set me off. I would then launch into this tirade about how lucky they are to be able to take piano lessons, and what a great skill they were acquiring if only they would make the commitment. The timer would finally sound, only to find me shaking from my tantrum and them teary eyed and hating the idea of having to learn to play the piano.

I decided, "No more." I made the decision that they were going to have great memories of mom helping them learn their piano; of helping them learn a skill that they will enjoy into adulthood. I made a commitment to make the time spent at the piano be more about them and me learning together, and less about perfection and time wasted. It's now a time of encouraging and applauding them, letting them share with me what parts they like and which ones they could do without. I've learned the different types of music that each of them prefer and enjoy, and have actually let them critique my playing of their assignments too! Before long, my oldest was voluntarily sitting at the piano and calling for me to come listen to the most recent song he had composed!

We are on our way to great mothering when we no longer measure how good a mom we are by the amount of time we spend with our children or by how well we have provided a loving home for them. We measure our mothering skills by the relationship that we have built and are continuing to build with our children. If you and I can build the friendship and relationship with our kids that my mom built with me, I believe we will have fulfilled our role as an awesome mom.

Relationship is the vision. Now let's start building.

~

We measure our mothering skills by the relationship that we have built.

~

# Chapter 3

## Mom, Are You Sure This Bridge Will Hold Me?

Here we are at LEGOLAND, and my family—Scot, kids, brother-in-law, sister-in-law and their children—and I have been waiting for the last thirty minutes to meet up with my husband's parents, who left at the exact same time. Understand that each of us family members have global positioning systems in our vehicles (which, by the way, is quite possibly the greatest invention of all time.)

Like I said, my in-laws have the GPS, so getting to LEGOLAND should be very simple. At that moment, my husband's cell phone rings and his mom starts telling him the GPS doesn't work. I can hear his dad in the background, yelling, "I will rip this system out of the car and throw it in the ocean! I will never buy a vehicle with a GPS again!"

This is funny because Scot is always talking and laughing about how his parents are "technologically challenged." His dad's cell phone, on which he has spent countless hours trying to teach him how to check his messages, now has a recording of him (Scot) that says, "Please don't leave a message, because my father, who can rebuild a Chevy 350-engine from the ground up, can't remember how to check his messages!"

So, now, his mom is saying, "This thing doesn't work." And Scot's trying to tell her, "All you do is type in 'LEGOLAND,' and it works." I can hear his mom telling his dad, "Tom, that's not how you spell LEGO. It's not L-O-G-O Land—it's L-A-G-O!"

What can you say? Every vacation needs a funny family story moment, but, seriously, sometimes the process of becoming an awesome mom is just like that.

We already "finished" being a great mom—in other words, we see the end result. Now we can start BECOMING an awesome mom. We have our destination; now we need our map. We need to know how to get there. We need to plug it into the GPS of life.

But first, let's find out where you are. Some moms may be well on their way toward a great relationship with their children, while others are wandering around in the land of having children who say, "I don't really understand or even like my mom!"

I have read books and listened to tapes that have had thousands of questions designed to determine what kind of mom you are. Some even include a test that you can take, and then by a score designed by who knows who, will attempt to give you further insight into just how you rank as a mom. But I have just one question. And the answer to this one question will tell you where you are right now and then point you toward where you need to be.

To find out where you are on the "mothering" scale, all you have to do is answer the question: "Do my children trust me?" Whether they are five years old or forty, do your children trust you?

## Building Trust Through Building Relationships

All you have to do is answer the question: "Do my children trust me?"

I am thinking about this very question as I am in my car with Peyton (my four-year-old son), and Matthew (my five-year-old nephew). They have been having a fairly in depth conversation on where babies come from, and Peyton has now posed a question to me. I begin to think that right now in his life, he trusts everything I say. If I were to say the sky is green and the grass is blue, he would believe me. If I were to tell him that babies are flown in from the stork, he just might buy it. However, this Matthew is a smarty, and he would never let that explanation fly!

Peyton doesn't doubt my love or commitment. In his heart, he believes that Mom can do and fix anything. There is no problem, no situation, no mountain too big for Mom, nothing that Mom is not capable of conquering. Mom knows all!

Right now, Peyton knows that unconditional love can be found by simply walking over to Mom and getting a hug. Security is just a bedroom away from where he sleeps. Acceptance is found in Mom's arms. Help is just a scream away. Finding happiness is as easy as saying, "Mom, will you play Uno with me?" Right now, everything is a little bit better when Mom is around.

So, that's why his innocent question has me holding my breath. I'm thinking maybe if I'm silent a beat too long, he will forget he ever posed the question at all. Maybe he'll assume that I didn't hear him, and then move on to talking to Matthew about something less heavy, like what happens when you hit puberty or something. Wide-eyed and more than mildly taken off guard, I continue to search the depths of my soul for an appropriate answer that won't leave him scarred after the birds and the bees talk in much later years to come. The whole "maybe if I'm silent thing" has not worked, and now my nephew is asking me to affirm what he has just explained to my little baby, my son so naïve and vulnerable to the ideas and knowledge of his much older and wiser friend. Understand that I'm not a person characterized by speechlessness, however, I've also never been so completely caught eavesdropping on a nearby conversation only to have them stop in the midst of said discussion to require my expertise, a conversation that is so much closer to the truth than they can possibly know or imagine, a conversation which has me giggling.

A conversation that went something like this: "Hey Peyton, did you know that your mom has a baby in her belly? And, did you know that she will have to go to the doctor to have the baby taken out? My mom has a baby in her belly, too. Yep, it's naked."

So far, Peyton's contribution to the exchange has been to bug out his eyes and nod in wonderment at his hero, his closest cousin and his best friend. But, the fact that Matthew thinks the baby is naked is too much for him to believe, so he responds to this by shaking his head, no. But, Matthew will not be denied his wealth of knowledge, so he continues. "Yes, it is. The baby is naked. Your mom will need to take some clothes to the hospital so that the baby doesn't come home naked. That's what they do, they bring the clothes to the hospital, so when the doctor pulls the naked baby from your mom, they have something for it to wear. And, then it's not naked anymore. That's how they get clothes. You were naked when you were in your mom's tummy, and she had to bring your clothes with her to the hospital."

At this point in the conversation, I have managed to obey all traffic signals and have broken no laws. However, Matt's next pearl of information has me swerving into the lane next to me. "Peyton, I know how the baby got into your mom." Please, do tell. "Seeds. Yep, your dad gave your mom seeds, and they are where the baby comes from."

Okay, so now I'm wondering just exactly how these discussions get started in my nephew's home. Do they begin over dinner? Is it during the salad course, or right after the main course? Or, maybe they save it for the good part, and bring it up during dessert? Either way, I am so wanting to call my sister-in-law right about now, but don't because I think we are still heading in a direction that may call for intervention on my part. "Yep, your dad has some special seeds, and when he gives them to your mom, they make a baby. A naked baby. It's true, ask your mom."

So, fast forwarding, you can see why I'm holding my breath. I could go with the seed thing, that is, the part that is more true than they know, but I'm thinking, "My little guy is so smart, what if he wants to know where dad puts them? What do I say then?" And, yes, the baby is naked, but that isn't really the part they are looking for me to confirm. Will they forget where they were? Not likely.

"Aunt Holly, didn't Uncle Scot give you seeds to make the baby in your tummy?"

Closing my eyes, yes, I'm still driving, I say, "Yea, babies come from seeds. Special seeds. Hey! Who wants a McDonald's Happy Meal?!"

It was just that easy. Onto bigger topics like, "Peyton, what do you think is better; honey with your Chicken McNuggets or hot mustard?"

You see, at age four, children believe whatever you say. They trust their parents. But one day Peyton will be thrown out into the real world. He will learn that you can't trust everyone. There are those out in the world who take rather than give, who hurt rather than love. There are those in the world who will not accept Peyton for who he is. But his mom isn't one of those people.

~

At age four, children believe whatever you say.

~

Peyton will have plenty of relationship disappointments in his life—friends who will stab him in the back, bosses who will treat him unfairly, women who will break his heart. There will be many people in Peyton's life who will not be trustworthy. But guess what? I won't be one of them.

That moment in the car, I made a commitment that Peyton would never have a reason to doubt me. Twenty years from now, I want Peyton to know that security is just one phone call away. Acceptance is still found in Mom's arms and words. And finding happiness is as easy as saying, "Hey, Mom, let's hang out today." Twenty years from now, I want everything to still be a little bit better when Mom is around.

Peyton—and all of my children—will always know that no matter what happens in life, Mom will be there to love, accept, help and guide them. This is a lifelong commitment. There is no point at which I can stop growing or can assume that my behavior doesn't matter.

Trust is something I hope Peyton will never have to question, because I will do everything in my power to assure him that I'm still the same woman he looked up to at four years old. When he's older, I want him to still be able to trust everything I say and have no question of my love. I want him to believe that unconditional love can still be found in a hug from Mom.

That is where I stand on the issue of trust. Now, be honest: Where are you on the issue? Do your children really trust you? "Sure, they trust me," you may say. To be sure, ask yourself, "Who do they go to when they have a problem, need something, or want advice?" Do they listen to you and trust what you have to say? If not, then you are lying to yourself.

You may wonder why trust is so important. It's important because it is the foundation of any relationship. No relationship will ever go beyond the level of trust. This applies to friendship, marriage, parenting—every relationship. If your trust level with someone is a two, then your relationship will never go beyond that level. How can you open up and share your dreams, desires, aspirations, and goals with someone you can't trust? Why go to someone for advice if you don't trust what he has to say?

Think about your own life. Think about someone who lied to you, broke trust with you, and then wanted to take the relationship to the next level. It couldn't happen—not until trust was reestablished.

If the relationship is the house you build, trust is the foundation. If the foundation is weak, the relationship will crumble, no matter how much time you put into it. You could be the nicest, funniest mom in the world. You could play games with your children, buy them everything they want, and tell them the best jokes. But if your kids can't trust you, all that time is wasted. No joke can overcome broken trust, and no amount of time spent together can build a relationship on a foundation of broken trust. Remember, time isn't the goal; relationship is. And to build a relationship, you must have a foundation of trust.

**Learning To Fly**

Trust isn't solely about building relationships. Having your children trust your word can save their lives. It can keep them from making huge mistakes. Sure, when your kids are little, they obey you because they have to. But sometimes in the teen years, they obey you because they trust you.

Raising kids is like teaching someone how to fly. In the beginning, the instructor sits right there next to you and can grab the wheel if you don't listen to the instructions or even land the plane if you get into trouble. But there comes a time when you are on your own, and the only advice you receive from your instructor is from the tower over the radio. Now whether or not you listen to the advice is determined by the level of trust you have in your instructor's words.

It's the same with children. When they're six years old, for example, you are right there next to them, ready to take that "wheel" if they get into trouble. You'll even land the plane if you have to! But then one day, those kids are in junior high and high school, and you are sitting out in the tower giving advice. "Don't hang around that crowd!" "Don't do drugs!" "Work hard in school!" "Go to college!"

But now that child has the choice to listen or not. Does he trust Mom's advice enough to listen? Or do his own desires or his friends' advice seem more trustworthy? Many teenagers have crashed the plane of life because Mom's words didn't ring true in their minds.

I don't know about you, but I want my children to trust me. I want them at age fifteen still coming to me for advice. Though they might not agree with what I tell them to do, I want them to trust me enough to still do it.

**Advice From the Wisest of Moms**

As I said before, trust will determine to whom your children will come for advice when they have a problem. Do they go to society or to Mom? Their trust in you will be the determining factor.

As Moms, how many times do we say, "If only my kids would listen to me—if they would just listen to my advice. I know what I'm talking about! Why won't they listen to me?" The reason is simple: The relationship lacks trust.

You say to your children that premarital sex isn't right, but their friends and society say there is nothing wrong with it. Whose advice do they trust? If the words of your daughter's boyfriend sound more true than yours, she could in end up in the backseat of his car.

You say, "Don't drink. Don't do drugs. They're dangerous addictions." But your kids' friends and Rapper "Big Bootie Two Crap" say, "There's nothing wrong with it. It's an awesome high." Whose advice do they trust? If their friends' advice sounds more true than yours, then alcohol and drugs will become a part of their lives.

~

Now that child has the choice to listen or not. Does he trust Mom's advice enough to listen?

~

What your kids do when you're not around is determined by the level of trust in you that you have instilled in their hearts.

**Doing What's Best for Others Builds Trust**

As a mom, we need to have a mindset of building trust. In everything we do, our hearts should be in this trust-building mode. We need to have hearts for what is best for our kids—not what is best for us.

Think about it. When you are looking for someone to baby-sit your kids, you want someone to take care of them the way you would. You want someone who will play with them, and make the time you're away fun for them. You don't trust someone who's just looking to make some extra money, someone who is only concerned with the amount of money you're going to pay them. You want someone who knows you're seeking what's best for your kids, and will do their best to be that. And when that sitter takes the time to really care for your kids, and see that they are doing well and having fun; that they are kept safe, over time, it builds a stronger and stronger trust between the two of you. But if they were to start neglecting your children, and not taking the right care of them, that trust is destroyed.

The same is true concerning the mother-child relationship. A mom who makes decisions based on what is best for herself will slowly tear down whatever trust she and the child have. But a mother whose decisions are best for the child will build a trusting relationship with those decisions.

**Trust Is the Bridge**

What is trust? To me, trust is a bridge built between two people that allows each to cross over safely into the other person's world.

Sure, many moms can see their kids' world—they can watch from a distance, but they are unable to cross over because of a poorly built bridge. They might be able to see their child heading down a wrong path. They can scream out across the bridge but it doesn't matter. The child can't hear his mom or doesn't want to hear her.

I want my children to feel like they can cross the bridge anytime for any need. My attitude is, "Please come into my world for anything at all. And please, allow me to speak into your world."

You see, for most kids, the bridge is old, worn out, and very shaky. On that first step across, a board may break underneath them. Maybe they came to Mom with a problem one time, and Mom started lecturing and nagging: "How could you even think about doing that?" Maybe Mom doesn't have time, and crossing the bridge isn't worth a child's effort. Maybe Mom never keeps her word. Because the child has no confidence in the bridge, he will not risk crossing it. He feels that chances are the bridge will break underneath him. Chances are he will take the long way and not go to Mom at all.

What would compel a child to try and cross the bridge into your world? An extreme emergency when he had to cross? Is that what you want? Or do you want your bridge to be strong so that your children never even question whether it will hold them? Anytime, anywhere, they know without a doubt, they can safely cross that bridge.

When it comes to your future relationship with your children, the bottom line is this: If a child can't trust you any more than his friends, then his friends, not you, will shape his destiny.

What kind of relationship do you have with your kids? Is it built on trust? Who will your children believe—you or some outside influence? On the roadmap of life, do you know where you are? You do if you understand that on the roadmap of the relationship you have with your children, building trust is one of the first and most important stops on your way to becoming a great mom.

# Chapter 4

## It's Time You Put Your Husband in His Place

Here's another great Scot story: "Here I am on the third day of watching the kids by myself. Not having slept in three days (since I stay up playing video games all night when Holly's gone), I am almost out of my wits. It is 8:35 a.m., and Laken starts kindergarten at 8:30. (Why this five year-old can't be more responsible is beyond me.) As I am rushing to get the kids into the van, Laken grabs an Avon® catalog off the driveway. He says, 'Dad, can I read this?'

"'Okay,' I answer hurriedly. In my day, an Avon® catalog just had makeup in it—maybe a few pretty girls modeling their blush or mascara—the worst-case scenario being a close-up photo of women's lips.

"So my mind, having gotten only two hours of sleep the night before, quickly computes the information: No harm; it will keep him quiet. And I blurt out, 'Yes, Son, you may read it.'

"Off we go to Laken's school, one that some might call a strict school of a certain denomination in which most everything in life is deemed as evil. Mind you, it is a very good school academically, one of the best in our state, but their biblical views are a little different from mine.

"I remember once, more recently, getting a call from Laken's second-grade teacher, who, by the way, is the daughter of the church's pastor, saying she was very, very concerned. I'm thinking, What did Laken do? Did he hit someone? Cuss? My goodness, is he smoking again? (That is a joke.)

"The tone of this teacher's voice made it sound to me like Laken was into some life-destroying habit. She says, 'Today, Laken… (there is a long, uncomfortable pause)…' Now, I'm really starting to be concerned. I'm thinking, Okay, what word did he say? #$%?! Or, #!$^? Whatever it is, this is big. I squirm a little, waiting for her to articulate Laken's dark sin. Finally, she stutters, 'He was singing a song from a movie. He was singing the song from *Shrek*! You know, the one about… I like big &#@% and I cannot lie?'

"Are you serious?!! No way! I finally respond with, 'We will deal with that.'

"Understand I'm not saying that the song is appropriate. I am saying that we blew the situation way out of proportion.

"I shared that to show you how strict a school this is. Again, I love the school. It's a great school. It's just a very strict school.

"Now back to Laken's being late to kindergarten. I should have known something was wrong because the kids were giggling during the whole trip to school. So I drop Laken off at school and take the two youngest kids home for naptime. At noon, we take off again to pick Laken up. As I'm driving, I can hear, from the back of the van, Heath, who was four at the time, giggling in a sinister tone. Actually, his laugh sounded similar to that of 'Beavis': 'Hrrr…rrr…rr.'

"We get to the school. I get Baylor and I say, 'Come on, Heath, get out of the van.'

"At which time Heath responds, 'Dad, look!' He then shows me a picture from this 'makeup' catalog of a half-dressed woman in lingerie. He laughs again: 'Hrrr…rrr…rr.'

"'Oh my gosh!!!' I say as I snatch the catalog out of his hands. I cry out with all that is within me, 'HEATH, YOU DON'T LOOK AT GIRLY MAGAZINES!'

"'Why not, Dad?' Heath asks.

"'You just don't do it. No, no, no!'

"'But, Dad, it was at our house,' he says.

"'I know that, Son, but this magazine is for big people to read.'

"'Heath thinks for a moment and says, 'So you can read it, right, Dad?'

His laugh sounded similar to that of "Beavis."

"'Yes, Son, Daddy can read this.'

"He accepts this answer and off we go to Laken's classroom. Standing outside the classroom are all the other parents, many of whom attend my church. The students are getting their backpacks on to go home. Laken is toward the back of the classroom. Out of nowhere, Heath screams out, 'LAKEN!'

"I look at Heath curiously, wondering what in the world he's doing. Laken screams back, 'WHAT!'

"And Heath screams, 'DAD SAYS WE CAN'T LOOK AT THE GIRLY MAGAZINE ANYMORE!!!'

"My jaws drop. Everyone turns and looks at us—kind of in slow motion. I look from face to face at the looks of shock and horror and I'm thinking, Why me, Lord? Just then, Heath screams out again, 'DAD SAYS ONLY HE CAN LOOK AT THE GIRLY MAGAZINE!!!'

"There were gasps from the crowd, and some parents pulled their kids close to them, as if I was some kind of 'sick-o' that might snatch them and run. At this point, I conclude that there is no way to explain what just happened. I have no words to offer. As everyone stares at the 'perv' and his children, we just walk away as, all the while, Laken is insisting, 'But, Dad, you said I could look at it!'

"'Yes, Son, you're right. I did say that," I answer as I vow that I will never let Holly go anywhere ever again."

I had just walked in the door from being "out." I had rewarded myself with some much needed girl time with some of my friends. And all I could do was stand in the foyer of my home and bite my lip to keep from crying. My house was a complete wreck!

Now, you're talking about a woman who obsessively purchases a tote for every type of toy my children own, a woman who has successfully, yet not without some purple hesitation, taught her children the value of the "clean up" song by Barney. But, here I stand in the middle of complete and utter chaos. I wasn't even sure that I could locate my husband and children due to the path of destruction they've left in their wake.

Had anyone, namely the husband, bothered to stop and evaluate what the state of the home might imply to me? All I could think of was how much effort it takes for me to keep our home looking good and organized. Of how not encouraging the children to pick up after themselves undermines so much of what I try to instill in them on a daily basis. The mess screamed, "WE DON'T RECOGNIZE, NOTICE OR CARE WHAT YOU DO! WE ARE WITH DAD, AND HE'S ALLLLL ABOUT HAVING FUN, FUN, FUN!"

Then the rage came, and I became the terminator. I began catapulting and hurdling over all the junk strewn throughout my pretty home in search of the man in charge! Finally locating him, I let go, let loose. You've been there, right? I just let it all run out, every last ugly, vulgar and very descriptive word I could find to describe my feelings in finding the place a mess! I didn't spare or consider his feelings in letting him know how inept, sloppy and completely irresponsible I thought he had been.

I don't know who came up for air first after that; or, for that matter, who walked away from whom. All I know is I ended up in my bedroom upstairs, alone, while he got settled in for the night on the couch.

I had just climbed into bed when the door to my bedroom creaked open, revealing two little boys in pajamas. "Mom?"

"Yes?"

"Are you mad at dad?"

"Yes."

"Why?"

"Because, the house is a mess."

"Mom?"

"Yes?"

"Dad didn't make the mess."

What do you do with that kind of logic? I mean, the three-year-old is making his best point in defense of his dad, but one which implicates wrong doing on his part. Honesty. Yes, his dad could and should have facilitated the clean up. But, I realized that that wasn't what my children had perceived when they heard us arguing. They knew cleaning up the toys was, ultimately, their job. They knew who had dragged the toys out and played with them. Still awake and having heard our argument, they were feeling responsible for the fact that their parents were seething mad at one another.

"Would it be okay if I slept with you and let Heath go sleep with dad so you aren't sleeping alone?" And, then whispering, "I made you mad at Dad."

There comes a point where the pettiness becomes so clear and the solution even more obvious. My boys needed to see us loving one another! They needed to see that moms and dads are humans, who will make mistakes and sometimes fight and argue, but most importantly, they needed to know that my love for their dad mattered more than my being right. And, let's face it. There is a mature way of saying things and getting our point across. I was and am eternally grateful to have a husband who willingly and without a second thought encourages me to have my girlfriend time often. I took both of my boys downstairs to witness me hugging and to their horror "smooching" on their dad, all the while, telling him I was sorry for overreacting.

Whether Mom is right or wrong—nice or not—it doesn't matter. Children want and need to know that their mom loves their dad.

~
I took both of my boys downstairs to witness me hugging and to their horror "smooching" on their dad.
~

To be a great mother, the most important thing you can do is love the father of your children. In fact, this is one of the best ways to start building that trust with your children.

Understand that in this chapter, I am speaking to women who are married to their children's father and to women who are not. It is a very difficult chapter to write and maybe more difficult to read if you are divorced. You must take into account what applies to your situation, realizing that my purpose isn't to make you feel guilty. Condemnation will never produce anything good. Instead, let's learn to be the best moms we can from that perspective.

Of course, it is easier and better for the children if Mom and Dad are married. That is just a fact: having Mom and Dad together is the best-case scenario. But that doesn't mean you can't raise great kids and have a great relationship with them if you're divorced. It just means more work because trust has been broken. Rather than continuing to break the trust, you can build it. The extra work it takes will be well worth the effort.

As a single mom, you will nullify all of your good intentions and hard work with your children if you talk badly about their father and don't love him unconditionally—not based on what he does or doesn't do, but because he exists. If for no other reason, you love him because he is the most important and influential man in your children's lives. In this, you know that love conquers all. He may talk badly about you to the kids. But you stay your course and speak only positively about him. One day, the truth will be revealed to the kids. They will grow up remembering all the times you spoke kindly regarding their dad, when maybe he hadn't given any reason to. You will have shown your children an amazing glimpse at true character and integrity. And, they will know you did it out of your love for them.

As a divorced mother, you should back your ex-husband up on the things he wants done with the kids. You make sure the kids respect and honor him. Teach your children to love their dad. In doing these things, you are building trust in your children, but you are also building trust in him. So when the time comes, and you and your ex don't agree on a particular parenting direction, it is the love you have given that will give you a window, an opening, to speak into his life. Over time, your love will build a trust within him that you do have the best interests of your children at heart. It will be this trust that, although you are divorced, will still allow you to guide and steer the family toward what is best for the children.

Besides, whatever the case, whatever the details of the divorce, leave the past where it belongs—behind you. There is a reason why a car's windshield is so much bigger than the rear view mirror. We should spend a lot more time focusing on what is ahead of us rather than what is behind us.

**First Things First**

Now, the first thing you need to do to build a trusting relationship with your children is to love your children's father.

Think of it from a child's perspective: How much trust can he have in a mother who talks down to his dad, who is rude to him, and who speaks negatively about him? How much trust can that child have in a mother who does not treat his father with a sense of respect, who does not value him? How much trust can he have in a mother who does things behind his father's back, a mother who doesn't back him up but only puts him down? How can a child trust a woman who does not love the most important man in that child's life?

All the fun time you spend with your kids and all your hard work to be a great mom is wasted if you're not a great wife first (or loving him as an ex). You cannot be a great mom unless you are a great wife—or, for single moms, you cannot be a great mom unless you love, not be in love with, but love unnconditionally, your children's father. Remember, it's about what that love is doing and building in your children that is really at issue.

**The Security of a Solid Marriage**

As I said, you cannot be a great mother until you are a great wife. This means that the husband-wife relationship has to be the priority relationship of the family. It is the heart of the family; it is what the children draw their security from. If the husband-wife relationship is not secure, the children will be insecure. Remember, we're still talking about trust—and insecurity is the opposite of trust. One way to instill security is by letting your kids know your marriage is secure.

Insecurity is the opposite of trust. One way to instill security is by letting your kids know your marriage is secure.

Imagine the sense of security they have when they head off to school, knowing in their hearts and having no doubt of Mom and Dad's love for each other. They know that divorce is never an option, that their mom and dad will do anything to work things out even if they do fight once in a while. Guess what? With that worry off their shoulders, kids can focus on school, friends, and being a kid. They can go forth confidently into the world.

But what if Mom and Dad are constantly talking about divorce? Nobody in the family knows if the marriage will last another day. And the fights are intense. This child takes the worry of what his world could become out into the world with him and is never free to just be a kid.

Perhaps you come from a broken home. What did it do to you when your mom and dad fought? Did you go into your room, pull the covers over your head, and cry yourself to sleep, praying that Mommy and Daddy would continue to love each other? Were you confused, upset, worried, and depressed, wondering what you did to cause this? What happened to your entire world? It flipped upside down. You couldn't be secure in the world because your world had no security. You couldn't be you because you made no sense. The insecurity of your parents' marriage brought pain into your world.

Now let's consider exactly what an unhealthy marriage does to your children's world.

Probably the most important need of your children is the need to know that you and your husband love each other. In fact, I'd be willing to bet that your children would give everything—all of their toys, everything—just to have Mom and Dad stop fighting. I actually counseled a young adult once who said that he would have even given up the love his parents had for him if it meant that they would love one another.

So you see, having parents who love each other is one of the most important needs your children have. Why is it that important? It brings a level of security to the home that a child needs to function confidently and securely in a very uncertain world.

You can certainly see the importance of working things out with your husband. We need to do whatever it takes to make the marriage work well. Understand that I am not talking about staying in an abusive relationship. By staying in an abusive relationship, whether physical or emotional, you are doing more damage than good. I am talking about the marriages that end just because the husband and wife fell out of love.

**Make Your Marriage a Decision**

Many people have said that life is about making right decisions. But I believe that even more importantly, it is about making decisions right.

Maybe it doesn't seem now like you made the right decision in marrying the man you married, but where life takes you from here is about making that decision right. See, you can spend the time working on the marriage, reading books, getting tapes, going to marriage seminars, growing and changing. You can spend the time investing in making your marriage amazing—and in time, it will be—or you can spend the time trying to fix the results of what a divorce brings into your life. One way or the other, I guarantee you will spend the time.

We all know people who didn't have the perfect marriage. They fought a lot when the kids were growing up. They were two different people forced to live one life, as with any married couple. That "loving feeling" wasn't always there. But what is it that makes one couple stay together and another one not? To that couple who stays together, divorce was never an option. They both worked hard at loving each other. They read books, listened to tapes, attended marriage seminars or counseling. Their children didn't go through all the junk some of their friends went through—all the fear and worry. And today, thirty-five or even fifty years later, they are best friends who are able to enjoy their family together and to look back at the huge mountain called marriage that they climbed together.

I don't think most women really think about what waits for them on the road of divorce. They don't think through what it will be like to have their children call another woman "Mom." What will it be like if the new mother has different attitudes and views about raising their children? What if the dad and new mom decide to move to another state? Then these women wouldn't see their kids during the summer and a lot of holidays. Another woman would do their job of mothering and have their time with those kids—time they could never get back. It's like I heard one little girl say when her parents got divorced: "I went from saying good night to my dad at night to saying good-bye."

If the decision to marry your spouse doesn't now seem like the right one, think about what it would be like to spend half of your holidays away from your children.

You'd go from tucking them into bed every night to seeing them off every other weekend. Maybe you don't get custody. Now, you might no longer be a part of their world; instead you might get to peek into their world every so often.

And what would it be like when your kids say, "Mom, please let Dad stay here tonight—please let him stay home." You'd have to explain to them that their home isn't Daddy's home anymore. With tears in their eyes, they might ask, "But, Mommy, who will protect us, who will watch over the house, who will be there if we get scared at night?" Explain to them then why Mommy doesn't love Daddy anymore.

I don't think most women really think about what waits for them on the road of divorce.

If at all possible, wouldn't it be better to make that decision right that you made during your marriage vows—the decision to love your husband "till death do us part?"

**Let Love Take the Lead**

The bottom line is that to be a great mom, you have to love your children's father. It is your responsibility to love him. Even if he doesn't love you, don't worry about him. You worry about what you can change—and that's you.

My mother-in-law once said something that stuck with both Scot and me. She said, "Life is about giving what you have so you can receive what you desire." Did you get that?

You see, if I desire love, I must give what I have, which is love. And when I give it, I open the way to receive what I desire. The problem most of us have is, we are trying to get love. But when you try to get it, you never receive it. When you give it, then it comes back to you.

Maybe you're saying, "But, Holly, he doesn't love me." Try for just thirty days to love him unconditionally. Throughout the day think only about the good things he does, give into him, do what this chapter talks about. In just thirty days you will see him start to love you back!

**Your Choices Produce Results**

Understand this: Results never precede choice—choices produce results. For example, I don't say I want a raise at my job, and then I will work hard. I have to choose to work hard, and that choice will produce a raise. Likewise, I could have the attitude that when my husband loves me, I will love him. No, I must love him first, and that choice will produce the result of him loving me.

Do you want a great husband? It is so simple.

Think back to the beginning of your relationship when you were in love. What made it different? Your choices. You chose to look beyond the bad, to look beyond what he did or didn't do for you. You chose to treat him like a king. When you were dating, you weren't so concerned with meeting your own needs. It was his needs that mattered. You worked hard to win his heart, and you acted as if you were the woman of his dreams, which made you the woman he wanted to spend his life with. You felt alive and so in love. You felt loved in return, so much so that you promised to spend your life with him. Why? Because you loved first.

But after the wedding, you stopped looking at your husband's needs, and you started focusing on your own needs again. You worked hard for your own heart instead of for his. Now you don't feel in love with him anymore. You need to go back to the point at which you felt love. Do what you did then, and I promise you, you will feel love again.

So picture this with me: Scot comes home from work one day, and, boy, am I mad. "Scot, I have had it!" I shout. "I have had it up to here with my insensitive actions toward you! I do not have sex with you enough. You should go going golfing more, and have more 'you' time! I am sick and tired of me not having dinner and laundry done! If I don't start loving you like I should, I'm out of here!" (This represents a typical fight that we all have had, right?)

What makes this scenario so facetious? I'm upset because I'm not meeting my husband's needs. But in real life, we are usually not upset over failing to fulfill our obligations. Rather, we are usually busy worrying about our husbands keeping up their end of the bargain.

Think about it. Isn't every fight you've ever had about him not meeting your need? Have you ever been mad because you were not meeting his need? I can almost guarantee that every single time you have ever been mad at someone, it is because your needs were not being met.

Think about a world in which people worry about others' needs and not their own. Imagine a marriage in which two people are more concerned about the other's welfare than they are about their own. If you will apply this to your marriage, you will have the best marriage since Adam and Eve. Why? Because once you eliminate self, you can put your spouse in his rightful place. What would there be to fight about? "I don't care what you say, Honey, I'm a control freak, and it ticks me off. I'm too angry at myself to talk right now…" You see, once you eliminate self, love steps in.

**Teaching Love by Example**

And do you know what else? By loving your husband unconditionally, you are also teaching your children what love really is and what should be expected in a loving relationship. You are explaining what love in action really is. How your kids love others when they grow up will in large part be determined by how you loved their father. For example, your sons learn what to expect from marriage based on what you expected. Your daughters learn how to love their future husbands based on how you loved their father.

Many women find themselves in abusive relationships, unwilling to leave. Why? Because they don't know there is anything different. This is how Dad treated Mom, so this is how my husband should treat me, they think. Mom put up with it; so should I.

Understand this: Your children need to see you lay down your life for their father. They need to know you will give it all up for him, that he is the most important person in your life. Your treating Dad like that solidifies a need children have inside, and when this need is met, trust is built. It's as if they're saying, "If I can trust you with my father, I know I can trust you with my heart."

Your children need to see you lay down your life for their father.

The funny thing is, this goes against what kids actually say. "Dad, come play with us," they whine. "Dad, why are you going out just with Mom? Take us with you! Why can't we all be together?" On the "outside" they are saying one thing, but on the inside dwells a need for Dad to make Mom number one, and Mom to make Dad number one. There is a bit of security that is placed in your children's hearts when they see Mom and Dad treat each other like the most important person in his or her life.

Being a great mom starts and finishes with being a great wife and loving your husband (or ex-husband). Making your husband your first priority gives your children a deep sense of security and trust from which they can go confidently into the world. And although love is a choice, the results experienced by your husband, your children—your whole family—will be tremendous.

# Chapter 5

## Eight Ways to Meet Your Husband's Needs: Sex, Sex, Sex, Sex, Sex, Sex, Food and Sleep

Scot and I, along with my dad, mom, brother and sister, thought it would be fun to take a vacation to visit my relatives in Ohio. We hadn't seen them since our wedding, and thought it would be a nice change before we embarked on one of the biggest journeys of our lives—parenthood. So, six and a half months pregnant and totally huge with my first child, we boarded a plane.

Now, awaiting our arrival in Ohio, were my aunt and uncle, my two older cousins, my one cousin's wife and their three children. Though I just shared that my cousin and his wife had three children, this particular story will be centered around their son Josh, who at the time of introduction to my husband was a great big whopping three years old. From the beginning to the end of this visit, I played referee so many times between the two that I began to believe that I was destined for the NFL.

Our visit to Ohio was a full seven days and nights, and was spent in what some could say was a battle. And all I can say is that Scot emerged. Not victorious, by any means, but not altogether conquered, either. He just emerged. He emerged from battle with little Joshie and lived to tell about it, while I, secretly, behind his back, live to laugh about it.

On Night One, the Joshinator, as Scot liked to call him, entertained us all by throwing a freshly buttered roll that hit Scot right in the head. At the time, Scot wasn't completely deserving of that, but there have been times throughout our fourteen years of marriage where I think it would have been really satisfying to chuck food his way. Scot claims it was a totally unprovoked attack, although, at the time and even today, I wonder. As Scot was wiping the butter off his face, all could hear the mischievous little laugh that still haunts him today.

When I'm asleep, I'm asleep. There is not much, short of dragging me from the bed, that can interrupt or wake me from my slumber. So, that's why I was skeptical to believe Scot's claim (spoken very respectfully in private) that, little Joshie made sure he was up at five o'clock every morning. Scot's claim was that Josh would bang on the door, give his signature laugh, and run. I felt so insensitive, but laughed anyway when Scot suggested that Josh truly had it out for him. "Anytime Josh has the chance, he hits me with the nearest blunt object he can find. Really, out of nowhere, he walks by and hits me in the shin, the knee, the head and twice has hit me in a more sensitive area." Scot seemed truly frightened and began to take inventory of every toy Joshzilla owned which could potentially be used as some sort of weapon to wear him down. "Even in the vehicle, I am not safe. Toys are being secretly launched from his seat in the van, fooling all of you into thinking that Josh has merely dropped his toy again."

But, Scot would not be pacified with explanation, still choosing to believe that Josh hadn't dropped the toy at all, but, rather had thrown the weapon, hitting him in the head. "You're a nut. Josh is quite possibly the cutest little boy ever, and you, my friend are delusional."

Even in the vehicle, I am not safe. Toys are beng secretly launched from his seat in the van.

As the week drew on, I found Scot taking great pleasure in little pranks against Josh. He would casually leave his leg sticking out as Josh ran by, would make goofy faces at him when he thought nobody was watching, hide his blanket and would actually take his favorite toys and hide them in our suitcase! "Do you have any explanation for how this toy ended up in my makeup bag?"

Excitedly, Scot would say, "Sshhh! He'll never find it in there! Do you hear him crying right now? I think he has noticed it missing!"

My response? "Grow up. I mean, exactly how old are you?" On one occasion he actually replied with, "HIM FIRST!"

On Day Five of the never ending battle, we all were invited to have dinner at my aunt and uncle's house. To fully grasp the humiliation I would suffer in this evening amongst family, you have to picture my aunt. She is the sweetest, most loveable person on the planet. It is Scot's belief that the only person one can possibly compare her with to give you a true picture is Aunt Bee from Mayberry because my aunt wore aprons and was always smiling and baking something. "Holly, Scot, do you want a cookie? Some cake? A piece of pie?" You spend two minutes with this woman and your soul craves a hug from her.

My Uncle Sherb, according to Scot, is by all accounts Andy Griffith, tall, quiet, kind, and oozes with the personality of a good listener.

So here we are at "Aunt Bee's" house, and Josh and Scot have already begun battle. A "trip" here—a toy jabbed in his back there. Finally, I see him get to a point of needing a break from his childishness. Under our own Geneva Convention, Scot felt we had an agreement that there was a place of refuge to which one could go—a free place, a happy place—where no battle was allowed. And for some reason I don't quite understand, this place, for Scot, was the bathroom.

So off he heads to the bathroom and, once inside, he turns to lock the door, only to find there is no lock on the bathroom door. I don't know why there is no lock (actually, I do know—it's because God has a sense of humor), but with the door decisively closed, he sits down.

And, it is while he is in this position, a most vulnerable position, that he claims he first heard the pitter pat of little footsteps coming down the hall.

Now, understand that much of the story taking place inside the bathroom is from Scot's personal account of what happened. You see, I didn't actually happen upon the scene until much later, when there was no hope for safe and dignified intervention. He claims that it was at this moment of hearing the footsteps, that fear gripped his heart. He says it was just like in the movies when a killer animal is approaching to finish the people off and they're hiding, hoping that if they're quiet enough, the predator will leave. But the animal never leaves, as you well know, because it smells fear. And so, says Scot, did little Joshie.

Scot heard Josh walk up to the bathroom. He said he could see his little shadow blocking the light from under the door. He sensed impending doom lurking on the other side of his dubious defense—the unlocked door.

Joshie paused. His heart seemed to stop. He said he could hear his own breathing, though he tried desperately to hold his breath. Finally, he heard Josh begin to walk away. Relieved, he felt his heart start beating again, and he says he exhaled a sigh of relief. It remained quiet for a few seconds when, all of a sudden, just like in the movies—boom!—the door swung open wide, and there stood Joshie in the doorway, buck-naked.

"I could tell by the expression on Joshie's face that in his three short years on the face of the planet, he had never encountered somebody being on 'his' potty when he had to go. I mean, it had never happened. By the look on his face, I could tell that he was very surprised. I, on the other hand, was very scared," Scot reported to me much later.

"We stared at each other for what seemed an eternity. I wouldn't blink because I remembered reading that if you stared an animal down, it would not attack. I just stared at Joshie, and he stared back until finally, he said (and he said it nicely), 'Get off my potty.'

"With trembling, I said to Joshie, 'I promise you, I am getting off your potty. Please close the door, and in two seconds, I'll get off your potty.'"

Scot's claim is that Josh would not be deterred, and replied, "Get off my potty."

Scot says he responded back to that with, "Please, Joshie. Please. You can go in just two seconds—one, two. I promise I'm going to get off your potty."

Then Joshie screamed, "GET OFF MY POTTY!"

Here's how Scot remembered what happened next: "That angered me because I knew he was going to attack. I was at the end of my leash. I thought, You wanna do battle, Joshie? Then let's do this! So with as firm a voice as I could muster, I said, 'Joshie, if you don't get out of here, I'm gonna bring it, Boy! And you don't want none of this! So get out of here now!'

"In hindsight, that was the wrong thing to say. Joshie let out a spine-chilling battle cry and screamed again, "GET OFF MY POTTY!" Then he charged me like an angry rhino.

"There I was, sitting down with my pants wrapped around my ankles—in as vulnerable a position as you can imagine—and I've got this angry, naked three year-old running at me. I began to seek God. "God, please help me. I need a miracle, an angel, something—anything. I'm not asking You to part the Red Sea. I'm not asking You for a mighty miracle. Just stop the charging naked boy, please! Get him out of here!"

> I was at the end of my leash. I thought, You wanna do battle?

He says he continued frantically, "Lord, give me something. Give me a scripture. The Word is supposed to be for every occasion. Give me a verse, some advice, some instruction—something!" He says he does believe he actually heard God in an audible voice say, "Turn the other cheek."

Continuing on as told by Scot, "So here comes Joshie, and he hits me with all of his force, nearly knocking me off the toilet. I regain my balance. He then tries to push me off, all the while screaming, 'Get off my potty! Get off my potty!' Still frantic, I say, 'Please, Joshie! Please stop!'"

I don't truly know what transpired in the final moments before the two boys were found, grappling like two wrestlers going for Olympic gold, but I do know we were all summoned, from dinner, mind you, by the sounds of things being thrown. Later I learned those things were pictures falling from the walls, a box of Kleenex, toilet paper rolls, shampoo bottle from the tub and, once or twice, Josh himself. Scot was trying to get his pants untangled and up, but said Josh kept grabbing his legs and his pants, pulling and pushing in a blind rage.

Now, who do you think is the last person in the world that I would want to see my husband half-naked? You guessed it—Aunt Bee. But there we all are, running. "What's going on?" she cries and then screams, "Oh my!" With the rest of us right behind her, I realize every relative has just gained a free ticket to the "Scottie Show".

Finally, someone breaks from the waves of laughter long enough to run in and grab little Joshie by the ankles. I believe it took more than one of them to drag him out, for he was really distressed by the fact that Scot, an adult, had not relinquished the use of this room which housed "his potty."

All said and done, Scot resorted to using the "potty" at the Circle K for the next two days.

Strangely enough, this chapter is about loving your husband. (Whether my family has seen him naked or not, I still love him.) In the rest of the chapter, I will cover seven ways to show your children that Dad is important. We've already established the importance of loving Dad. In this chapter, we will discover how.

In essence, there are seven ways to build trust in your children's hearts through loving their father. Again, if you're a single mom, do not dismiss this chapter as if it isn't for you. You need to be practicing these same principles for the father of your children. Remember, your children learn the very meaning of love from the example set by their mom.

**Number One: Sex, Sex, Sex**

Let's just get this one out of the way. Your man needs sex. He almost needs it more than he needs food or air. A happy husband starts and ends with sex. There you have it; you can deny it, ignore it; it is still true. If you want to love your husband, give him sex, really good sex.

Isn't it interesting that we expect our husbands to become good at what is important to us? For most women that is conversation. What would happen if your husband only had conversation with you once a week? (Sadly this might be true for some. You need to set some boundaries in this relationship.) Let's say in that once-a-week conversation he acted like he hated it, acted like he wanted it over quickly. "Can we just make it a quickie get it over with?" He just sits there and takes it. What if he went weeks without talking to you at all? Just like most of us need that conversation time, he needs intimacy. He needs really good sex. Why not become amazing at it? If it is that important to him, make it important to you. Get some books on it. Find out how. Lets be honest. No one trained us how to be great, we just learn.

Whether you know it or not, your husband talks about his sex life with his friends, a sex life that includes you. "Oh, no he does not!" you may say, but I would almost guarantee you he does. Most men talk about how often they do or don't get this need fulfilled, whether they come right out and say it or simply imply it. Regardless, I desire to be the woman who gives her husband reason to brag (not literally, or in detail, for he knows that is a really great way to end his fulfillment). It's a good goal, though, to recognize and fulfill a need that is very real and very much part of a man's make up. Why not become the best at something that is so important to him? You know when you give your heart to something, it becomes so much better even for you. Don't dump it before you have truly given it your best effort!

I know as a mom we get so busy throughout the day that sex is last on our mind. Now, don't share this with your man (and I won't share it with mine), but I had a really great woman, married and loving it, share with me on the necessity of sex for a man in marriage. She said that most women struggle with the switching from "mom" mode, into "sexy wife" mode. Early in her marriage, she decided that she would make this a priority, and without telling her husband, she would mentally schedule the days that she would initiate intimacy. On these days she would plan how and when she would make her move. She related that the thinking on it, and being creative in the ways that she set the mood, had her anticipating the switch from "mom" mode to "sexy wife" mode.

~

Most women struggle with the switching from "mom" mode into "sexy wife" mode.

~

I challenge you to spend a few moments in the day thinking about it. Go ahead and decide how you would like to set the mood. Maybe plan his special dinner, and put on your favorite dress, and one that he likes, too! Maybe surprise him and have the kids with a sitter, and a picnic dinner waiting for him and you in the bedroom, on the bed. Or, maybe you just take every opportunity from the time he gets home till you put the kids to bed to hug or kiss him; letting him know the attraction. Most of the time, sex is done out of duty. Make it something fun and exciting, and you'll find yourself initiating and indulging more often. Rather than putting in "one more hour" at the office, you'll have him racing home to see you.

**Number Two: Give Him Priority**

One of the most important ways to show your kids your love for their dad is to give him priority. Dad has to get the best, particularly of your time.

When he gets home from work, the first fifteen minutes of your time belongs to him, just as his first fifteen minutes home belong to you. The point is that the two of you take time to share about your respective days. And, this is an opportunity for your husband to fulfill your need for some adult conversation. (Encourage your husband to read Scot's book, because it is important that both of you do this, and his book explains its merits to the man.) It is the best of your time, and your children need to see it given to Dad. The kids will likely say, "C'mon, Dad, play with us! Talk to Mom later." "No, Mom and Dad's relationship is really important. I've missed your dad, and I am going to spend some time talking with him right now."

I know you probably want him to go play with the kids, give you a break, and he can after the first fifteen minutes, but it is very important that the kids see the husband/wife relationship ranks number one. The kids may outwardly show signs that they don't like it, but inwardly it confirms what they need. It establishes that sense of security in knowing Mom is first in Dad's life, and Dad is first in Mom's life. If you wait until the kids are in bed to give time to the relationship, the kids don't get to visualize the importance of the relationship. Do not underestimate the power of such a little thing! It's just fifteen minutes, but each of those minutes is building trust in the heart of your children. And they will affirm verbally much later in their lives how they loved that you loved their dad, and let them know it.

**Number Three: Meet His Needs**

Outside of sex, your husband has other needs that must be met. In a lot of ways men are easy. They need sex, sleep and food. Indulge intimacy, make him a sandwich, and let him take a nap. He is good for another twenty-four hours.

But men do have deeper needs. We need to realize them, and then honestly attempt to meet them. "Well, he isn't meeting my needs!"

He may not be, but you can't change him; you can only change you. And many times men are saying the same thing in response to why they aren't. "SHE isn't meeting my needs." Someone has to go first. Try meeting his needs. Become the best wife possible. Most of the time, he will change right along with you. If he is reading Scot's book, then he should be changing on his own. (If he isn't reading his book, give him need number one after every chapter he reads. Done right, he might finish the book tonight!) Now if your husband isn't changing, well now it is time to get the book called *Boundaries* by Dr. Henry Cloud and Dr John Townsend. Set some expectations in the marriage for what he will do. But for now, let's change what we have the power to change—ourselves.

A man can be this big macho, egotistical, testosterone-filled being. But behind this charade, is a little boy who wants you to be proud of him. He wants you to assure him, value him and think he is the greatest man in the world. A man's ego probably is the most fragile thing in the universe. Often times it takes just a comment to shatter this thing. Behind every successful man is a woman, a woman who built him up, who cheered him on, and who got him off his sorry butt when he needed it. Your man needs that pat on the back when he does a great job. He needs to hear you say how proud you are of him. Your children need to hear you say it to him, in front of them. If your man is confident, he can take on the world. If he is unsure of himself, he will take down the world around you.

This doesn't mean you have to be his cheerleader. I know many women who spend their life trying to cheer up their man, trying to make him happy. The only one that can make him happy is himself. I see women pouring into this black hole of poor me, and why me, just to get nothing in return. That is not what I'm talking about. These women need to tell their husbands, "Get happy, get out there and make some things happen. You are a smart man, and you can be very successful, if you get off your butt and do something." In a way, you are pushing him to excellence. Notice how I didn't use negative words. I motivate him by sharing his positives characteristics. It really comes down to the concept of balance. We don't give our husbands their worth and value. We affirm and encourage the worth and value that is already in them. I understand and agree that one thing women really find attractive in a man is confidence, that self-motivation that has them striving to be their best. It's frustrating when the expectation to create that characteristic in them is placed as a responsibility of the wife. However, many men have started off in marriage confident and motivated only to have it go unnoticed, unappreciated and unaffirmed to the point of losing said confidence and motivation.

Behind this charade is a little boy who wants you to be proud of him.

My mother-in-law tells a story of her husband. She put him through college. He got his teaching degree, and then he decided to keep working sheet metal. She said, "Oh no, you're not. You have come too far with this goal, and you can finish it!" She encouraged him as he mailed out thirty resumes all over the state. Within two weeks he had a teaching position. When he got laid off at age forty, she was right behind him, saying, "You can do it. We believe in you." When he was sent out to fail at age forty-five, she stood by his side. The two of them, together, built one of the largest churches in America. Realize that you and your husband can do great things, but it takes boundaries, agreement on goals, encouragement, giving honor and value.

Ladies, let's build up our men. When he leaves for work, make sure you set him up for success. If he leaves thinking you are mad at him, or you don't believe in him, he will struggle throughout the day. But if he leaves knowing you are behind him, you believe in him, there is nothing he can't do. Put yourself in his shoes. We like to be affirmed in our endeavors; so do they. And if he isn't leaving for work, let him know he better get up and start! You have expectations and goals, and he is capable of great things. (If you find yourself with a hubby who expects you to carry the family, I highly recommend the *Boundaries* book). What you speak to him and expect from him will help create the world in which you live.

Next thing on his list of needs is that we pay attention to how we look for him. We don't have any problems when it comes to getting dressed up to go out with the girls, to go out with friends, or go to church. But, how often do you find, when considering what to wear for him, you've chosen to throw on some jeans and a t-shirt? We all have those "ball cap" days, but are those days your norm? We should dress to impress our man. More often than not, we should have him thinking and saying, "WOW!" You are going out on a date, he should say, "WOW!"

Men love to walk down the street with their wife all dressed up and looking fine. So do we! We love when they are looking good, all physically fit, dressed for our eyes only. Somewhere along the way we have gotten confused and attached to a mindset that says that men are completely different than women. But I disagree. There are many topics on which both genders place the same importance and value. Whether he says it or not, it is very important to him. I have counseled many women who have said, "He doesn't look at me like he used to." Well, give him a reason to look. It just might be time to go shop for some new lingerie! Not sure of his favorite color? Take him with you!

Here are some other important needs men have, but more importantly your kids need to see.

At Christmastime, some moms and dads will decide to buy presents just for the kids. Let me just say that moms are the greatest, because they have no problem giving up everything for the kids. That just proves how much more they deserve gifts. Dads often times want to do this to save money. That is not okay!

I know, having discussed this with my husband, that to a man's mind, it makes sense to spend that money on the kids. But, in the kids' hearts, they need Mom to be treated like a queen and Dad to be treated like a king. Once again, the marriage relationship is the most important relationship. She comes first and he comes first. You should spend at least as much on Dad as you do on each child. (He should do the same for you. Hopefully he is reading Scot's book.) Why? So the kids can see what he means to you, and what you mean to him. Kids don't always understand what they hear; they are sight-oriented. Dad says he loves her, but what does he get her for Christmas, Mother's Day, and her birthday? Does he ever just surprise her with gifts? Who does the shopping? Does he send the kids on these errands? Mom says he is important, but he got nothing for Christmas or his birthday. I understand men often times ask the wife not to buy him anything or will say they don't want or need anything, but, you need to tell him, "Sorry, Honey, this is for the kids' benefit. You are getting something nice, and you will like it."

"What if I don't have the money?" you ask. Scrimp and save all year if you have to. If you put away $3 a week, in one year you could buy a really nice gift. Skip three Starbucks trips a week (over $600 right there). What is more important, Starbucks or him? Okay let me rephrase that. Show him you think he is more important than Starbucks. Or, give up one fast food lunch every week ($400 a year), and you now have the money to show your kids what Dad means to you.

It is also your job to make sure your children realize Dad's needs. It is your responsibility to teach your children to love him and to treat him like a king. Kids are naturally selfish and self-motivated, and they need to be trained to love. You should be asking them, "What are you getting Dad?" And then you should be telling them, "Okay, you have the best dad in the world; he makes sacrifices every day for you. So you can do better than that. Father's Day is coming up, and we need to make it special."

My mom always made sure my siblings and I bought our dad a gift.

There's nothing wrong with telling your kids on the weekends, "Let your Dad sleep in. Let's take him breakfast in bed to thank him for all that he does and for being the best. Kids, today is all about Dad."

My mom always made sure my siblings and I bought our dad a gift. She made sure it was nice. She would take us out before Father's Day, and have us spend our own money on it. It taught us to value Dad. And it showed us that she valued Dad.

When you're teaching your kids to meet Dad's needs, make a time of it. I take all four of our kids to the mall and let them pick something out and buy it with their own money. They go from store to store, looking for the perfect gift for their dad. Sure, it takes about two hours, but what it puts in them will last a lifetime. I believe a lot of kids grew up in good homes, but were never taught how to love or to give back. So from the teenage years on, they never gave back to the family. Though the family gave their all to them, Mom and Dad never trained them to give back.

I remember one Mother's Day, Baylor had it in his heart to buy me this ceramic dolphin figurine. Now, I have many interests, but the animal kingdom is not one of them. Sea World is probably one of the last choices on my personal list of vacation hot spots. This is the first and only figurine I own that is connected to animals in any way. But this gift has been displayed for all to see on a counter and was later moved to a special spot on my bath tub. It was Baylor's own money that purchased this gift for me.

To see Baylor's face—that he was so proud of the gift he'd bought—filled my heart with joy. Baylor said excitedly, "Mom, you can put him right here [on our kitchen table] so everyone can see him." And that is where that gift remained for a long while. It was a reminder that I was deeply loved.

Esteeming Dad with gift-giving and teaching your children to love him and meet his needs is your job. This goes for single moms, too. Make sure that your kids are loving Dad when you're not around. You should still take them out for holidays to get Dad a gift. You may say, "But he doesn't deserve it; hehasn't earned the right to be made to feel special." So what? If you want your kids to live a long life, it starts by honoring Dad. If you want your kids to learn to love back, it starts with you teaching them to give. If you want your children to trust you, it starts by loving the father of your children.

**Number Four: Never Let Divorce Be an Option**

The fourth thing you can do to show your kids that you love their father, is to make sure they know that divorce is never an option. It is simply never even discussed or brought up. Once it becomes an option, it is only a matter of time before it becomes a reality. Threats of divorce bring only insecurity to your children and to the relationship. And what we're trying to build is security and trust.

Conflict is a normal part of relationships. You get two people in a house together and you will have conflict at some time or another! You might fight, but if your kids know that divorce is not an option, your fights will not bring insecurity to their world.

Let's be honest—we never want to fight in front of our children. But I know for myself that, in reality,

Scot will say something stupid sometime this year, and Scot and I will probably fight. We try not to do it in front of the kids, but we know they are okay if it happens from time to time. Actually, if we are able to work through disagreements and conflict the right way, our kids can learn how to work through disagreements and conflict in their own lives.

Scot and I fight once in a while. I call it "sharpening iron" when we do. I read a great book once that said, "As iron sharpens iron, so a man sharpens the countenance of his friend." You can't sharpen iron without having a whole bunch of sparks! Scot and I sharpen the daylights out of each other. But it's all part of growing, changing, maturing and learning how to act in the relationship until the day comes when the husband and wife are two sharp pieces of iron who rarely need any re-sharpening.

Normal fighting doesn't bring insecurity, especially in light of a very verbal and public apology that the children observe, but talking about divorce and leaving does. Choose today never to use those words, never to speak them. Don't even talk about taking a break from each other; no, you need to sharpen each other. You may remember the saying, "Do not let the sun go down on your wrath." When you and your husband experience conflict, you make sure you work it out before you go to bed.

All it takes is one time for you to say divorce is an option, and, just then, a seed of insecurity gets planted in the hearts of your children. Now, if you have already done this, you sit down as a family, apologize, and affirm to one another that divorce is never an option. Show your children that you are committed to working through disagreements.

You can't sharpen iron without having a whold bunch of sparks! Scot and I sharpen the daylights out of each other.

**Number Five: Go on Dates!**

The fifth thing you can do to show your kids that Dad is the love of your life is to go out every week together. Now, for many women, the lack of this falls on the husband's inability to recognize its importance. However, there are many moms, be honest, who can't seem to pull themselves away from the kids; feel guilty leaving them behind with a babysitter while they go enjoy a night out on the town, or maybe you "can't find a babysitter I trust."

Stop making excuses, and begin making priorities! The kids will someday leave and follow goals and dreams. Where will you find your marriage? Will you recognize the man you married? Will you still want to know him? Will you be stepping into another awesome phase of sharing life, or will you wonder what exactly it is that you have in common? Again, your kids may fuss, cry, whine and moan, but deep down, the security you are giving them far outweighs their fear that you don't enjoy, love or want to spend time with their dad.

I believe in going out every week if possible and taking at least one trip a year, just you two. If your relationship is important and the heart of the family, treat it like it is. You need to make time alone together a priority. Now it is his job to make sure it happens, not yours. But, if you're not already doing this, sit down with your husband and share how you're feeling, that you value and need time with him. Share what impact you think it could make on your relationship and the kids. Set up an expectation; some boundaries in the relationship. Once again, if he does not rise to the occasion get the book Boundaries.

Also, let your kids know that Dad is taking Mom out. Our kids usually object: "Dad, Mom, take us, too!" We tell them, "I love you so much that I won't take you." They don't understand that, but my point is, I love them so much that nurturing the husband/wife relationship is more important than making everything be about the kids.

Don't get all caught up with the idea of everything being about the whole family. When the kids move out, it will still be just you two. If you don't build a relationship, or if it is built around the kids, one day it will fail. And a divorce when your kids are adults is equally as hard on them.

"Well, Holly," you may argue, "money is tight, and we're too busy to go out, just the two of us." Hey! We have all been there. We have all been through a time where money was tight. But, "going out" can equate to so many things. Maybe you go to your favorite restaurant and share a dinner. Public parks and picnics are always a great way of spending some inexpensive quality time. Go ride bikes, stop in at a coffee shop, walk through model homes, go people watching at the mall; you get the idea. The point is that you get out, together, without the children. There will always be better ways in which we could spend the money, but is it worth doing so at the expense of our children's being secure in the fact that their parents love one another?

"But, Holly, baby-sitting is expensive!" Then find another couple to switch baby-sitting with. You watch their kids one week, and they watch yours the next. Get rid of cable TV, high-speed Internet, fast food, sodas and that gas station cup of coffee every day. That's enough money right there to go out for a nice date every week. A great relationship with your husband will bring much more joy to your life than cable TV and a Big Mac.

**Number Six: Voice Your Commitment**

The sixth important way to love your husband is to voice your commitment to him. It is very important for your children to hear you say how much you love their father and what a great husband you think he is. Confirm what they know in their hearts—that you are blessed to have him.

Tell your children your dating stories and share all the good times you had and are having with the man of your dreams. Make sure they hear how much Mom loves the most important person in their lives, their dad.

When your children are older, think about renewing your wedding vows. Let them be a part of the ceremony so they can hear the commitment you make to each other all over again.

If you're a single mom, tell your kids how blessed they are to have their dad. Tell them what a great person he is. Teach them always to see the good in him. Never talk badly about him and never put him down. If you do, with every negative word about their dad, you chip a little bit of trust away from your own relationship with your kids.

**Number Seven: Show Him Affection**

The seventh way to show your kids how much you love their dad is to show him affection in front of them.

Voicing your commitment to him is one thing but demonstrating it is another. Your children want to see you kiss. Your older kids may say, "Get a room!" but inside, it is confirming what they want to know—that Mom cares. They like to see their parents hug and hold hands in public. But make sure you're not just doing these things for outside show; do them all the time.

**Number Eight: Agree With Him**

The eighth best way to love your husband and build trust with your kids is to agree with your spouse. In other words, back him up. Kids will play you and your husband against each other if they can. They'll ask Mom first for something they want. If they get the wrong answer, then they'll ask Dad. One of the greatest things you can give to your children is agreement with your husband. When you and your husband are in disagreement, the kids in a sense win because they get what they want. But they actually lose because they don't get what they need.

Kids will play you and your husband against each other if they can.

When my kids ask for something, I'll say, "What did Dad say? If you asked Dad, don't ask me." I back him up. And if you don't agree with one of your husband's decisions on something, never say it in front of the children. Back him up in front of them and then talk privately. Then you can make it look as if he changed his mind. But never undermine his authority. It is your job to strengthen his authority, not weaken it, in the eyes of your children.

Your mindset should be to make your husband look good. As moms, we are to back Dad up. We are to build him up and take his side. In this, we build trust in our relationship with him and in our relationship with our kids.

Dad's value in the home needs to be esteemed. So protect and uplift his needs to the children. Never allow the kids to talk badly about their dad. Your job is to always point them to the good, to see the good things he does. He is your Prince. Nobody, including your kids should ever be allowed to talk bad about him.

This also goes for single moms. Make sure you always speak well of him to the kids, and make sure they do the same. Even if he is a jerk, in the end, it builds trust in the hearts of your children.

I hope you can see that these eight ways of loving your husband are the building blocks of establishing trust in your home—trust that begins in your marriage and that translates into confidence and security for your entire family.

# Chapter 6

## Living a Life Of No Regrets

Here we are on our family vacation to San Diego. Scot's parents have rented all of us the beach house of the year. This house has all the amenities of the rich: computer light switches, a 20'-by-20' sliding door that opens the house to the beach, plasma TVs, a home movie theatre, a swimming-pool sized bathtub that you can do laps in, and so forth.

So here I am, unpacking, while Scot is bringing all forty-three bags in from the van to the house. On about trip thirty-seven, Baylor, my four-year-old at the time, says to Scot, "Dad, you just have to see the sink in the bathroom! It's just my size!"

I think to myself, now that's accommodating kids. I mean, who designs a bathroom tailor-made to a children's size unless you are a daycare? Scot nods to Baylor and continues his back-breaking getting-settled-in routine. Baylor continues, "Come and see it, Dad! You too, Mom!"

I suggest that we should let Dad finish bringing in the luggage first because he still has about seventeen more trips to go before he is truly done. Baylor keeps insisting, "But, Mom, I can sit on the toilet and wash my hands at the same time! I want to show Dad!" I walk away amazed at Baylor's favorite beach house amenity while in the back of my mind wondering, don't these people realize how fast children grow?

Finally, Scot brings in the last of the bags; the scrapbook bag I didn't truly need. He throws it (thinking I'm not paying attention to what he's doing) against the wall. Just then, Baylor cries out, "Come and see the sink, Dad!"

I have never seen my son so excited about anything, so we both head upstairs and turn the corner just in time to see Baylor sitting on the toilet and washing his hands in a bidet. He exclaims, "Dad! Mom! You can even get a drink out of it…"

We scream in unison, "Baylor, NO-O-O-O-O!"

If you boil life down to what really matters, you will find that what matters most will be that thing that you want most to have at the end of your life. No woman on her deathbed has ever said, "I wish I had spent more time cleaning and doing the laundry. I wish I had spent more time with my Bunco group. I wish I had watched one more *Grey's Anatomy* episode. I wish I had a couple more useless Hollywood gossip tidbits clouding my mind."

No, most women would say, "I wish I had spent more time with my family. I wish I had invested more into my children. I wish I had different memories of my time with my husband and kids. I would give anything to spend one more day at Disneyland watching my children's faces light up, to watch them one more time running through the waves in the ocean."

Listen closely, ladies: Life really is about creating memories.

I want to have great memories of what I've done with my family. You see, when the kids move out and go live their own lives, what I have left of their childhood is the memories of times spent with them. When you look at life like that, it changes how you approach every single day. You'll get up with the thought, How can I make a memory today with my family? Or, What type of memory will I be making today?

Life really is about creating memories.

You'll get home from running around and figure out what kind of memory you can make with your kids in the time before they have to go to bed. Do you make the memory of Mom getting right on the phone—which could be just one great block of memory that will stick with them—or do you make a memory that brings a smile to their faces, a memory of time Mom invested in them?

Realize that what you do with your children, the memories you build with them, will carry on for generations to come. I share stories with my children of the priceless memories I have of times spent with my mom and our family. What's amazing is that we often don't realize how the smallest of gestures, the simplest of times, can create a lifetime memory.

For example, I can remember almost every time my mom had us jump in the car for a "Jack-in-the-Box" nacho run! I can remember every single vacation we ever took—from the camping trips at the various lakes, sunburned and dirty, to the freezing ones in the woods where we huddled with each other in search of warmth! I remember the trips to California where our destinations were places like the beach, Sea World, and Disneyland! I especially remember the fact that we never called ahead; we just searched for whichever motel had room for thirteen kids and two adults. (Yes, I said thirteen kids. Not related, but still a family; a book to be written at a later date.)

I remember the trip to the Grand Canyon. We drove five hours to get there, stopping at cool spots along the way. It made us realize that there is more to Arizona than we thought. I remember being in complete awe at how beautiful the Grand Canyon was, especially as the sun was setting, thinking of how small it made me feel, yet so surrounded by good things.

I remember the trips to Grandma's house, and the many weekends spent with family, alternating whose house was host. I remember the birthday parties, the awesome Christmas Eves spent with lots of cousins, aunts and uncles, grandparents and all the other holidays in between. My mind is full of all the great memories we had while growing up. There are so many good ones that they overshadow the not so good. In fact, I can't even remember very many negative ones that happened to creep in during my growing-up years.

Moms, it is so important that we remember to create memories. It's not the kids' job—it's ours! You see, if you create memories and invest time when your kids are young, when they get older, they will still want to create memories with you as well as create memories with their family when they have one. The mom who sits around complaining about how her kids never visit anymore, doesn't realize that it may be her own fault. If she didn't sow any great memories into her family, train her children that it's vitally important to do so, it will be impossible to reap any great memories as a harvest, they haven't been taught or trained to do it back, or desire it.

The world operates under the principle of sowing and reaping. You may have heard it as "What goes around comes around." If you sow time into your kids when they're young, you will reap time with them when they're older.

It is true that when your children are younger, it's hard to play games with them, knowing that there is just so much more that needs to be taken care of, and, to be honest, sometimes playing those games isn't much fun for us adults. There are many things we would rather be doing than that. We're tired, worn out, in need of time alone. But then when our children are teenagers and can play all the really fun games, are able to help us out and lighten our load by doing some of the things they couldn't when they were younger so that we have some time to relax and enjoy, there are a lot of other things they would rather be doing than spending time with their parents! But if Mom created a habit in them, as we saw in Chapter One, if she sowed time into them when they were young, they will desire to see the time and memories continue.

Do you remember that Harry Chapin song "Cat's in the Cradle"? That song, in a nutshell, perfectly captures the sowing-reaping cycle of parenting.

*A child arrived just the other day.*
*He came to the world in the usual way.*
*But there were planes to catch and bills to pay.*
*He learned to walk while I was away.*
*And he was talking 'fore I knew it, and as he*
*grew,*
*He'd say, "I'm gonna be like you, Dad.*
*You know I'm gonna be like you."*

*And the cat's in the cradle and the silver*
*spoon,*
*Little Boy Blue and the Man in the Moon.*
*"When ya' comin' home, Dad?" "I don't*
*know when.*
*But we'll get together then.*
*You know we'll have a good time then."*

*My son turned ten just the other day,*
*Said, "Thanks for the ball, Dad. C'mon let's*
*play.*
*Can you teach me to throw?" I said, "Not*
*today.*
*I got a lot to do." He said, "That's okay."*
*He walked away, but his smile never dimmed.*
*He said, "I'm gonna be like him, yeah.*
*You know, I'm gonna be like him."*

*Well, he came from college just the other day*
*So much like a man, I just had to say,*
*"Son, I'm proud of you. Can you sit for a*
*while?"*
*He shook his head, and he said with a smile,*
*"What I'd really like, Dad, is to borrow the*
*car keys.*
*See you later—can I have them please?"*

~
If she sowed time into them when they were young, they will desire to see the time and memories continue.
~

*I've long since retired. My son's moved away,*
*I called him up just the other day.*
*I said, "I'd like to see you if you don't mind."*
*He said, "I'd love to, Dad, if I could find the*
*time.*
*You see, my new job's a hassle and the kids*
*have the flu,*
*But it's sure nice talking to you, Dad.*
*It's been sure nice talking to you."*
*And as I hung up the phone, it occurred to me,*
*He'd grown up just like me.*
*My boy was just like me.*[1]

Now, what is that song about? Regret! It is about a man who today regrets the relationship he has with his son. He regrets the time he missed out on because he was too busy to invest time in his son. He regrets not having good memories in life. Though the song is about a man, it is just as applicable to moms.

This chapter is about you living a life of no regret.

I was reading an article a few years back about regret. In it was a survey of men and women between the ages thirty-five to sixty-five. More than eighty percent of them had a considerable amount of regret in their lives. In men and women over the age of sixty-five, more than ninety percent of them had a considerable amount of regret.

I imagine that they regretted their relationship, or lack of one, with their spouses or they regretted the way their children turned out. Maybe they regretted not having much of a relationship, or many memories, with their children.

Once parents' kids are out of the house, a mom may be left having nothing: no memories of family times together, no memories of vacations together. Sure, at that time in their lives, she kept the house clean and laundry washed and folded, but that was a never ending need that wasn't going anywhere had it been put off for a few hours to enjoy her kids. Had she invested that same time and thinking into the family, she would have had thousands of priceless memories to treasure once the children were gone. Sure, that mom put many others to shame by having the cleanest house and best-dressed kids, but she wasted that time on tasks that today don't seem so important anymore. Sure, she can tell you what is the best way to remove stains from a particular fabric, but finds she can't tell you the hopes and dreams inside the hearts of her children.

Wasted time spent away from the family, doing things that later mean nothing, is a major problem in America today. I don't want to live a life of regrets. I don't want to be one of those Americans who possesses nothing more than memories of time wasted on myself and on what I considered to be the pleasures of life. I want to be 110 years old, living a life of no regrets, looking at my spouse and knowing that I spent wisely the time given to me on the earth. Scot will still be my best friend. I know one of us will have to die first, but I hope it will be me, because I can't imagine one minute without the man I love. Scot and I have millions of memories of time spent together because he has made sure we go out on a date every single week. He makes sure we take a couple of mini vacations, just the two of us, every year. He makes sure that when he gets home from work each day, I get the first part of his night, talking and sharing about life and our respective days. Moms, it's important that you do not feel guilty or worried about leaving your children so you can have the time with your spouse that your marriage needs! Many women live through the lives of their children; they get their value and their worth from being a mom. But, your motherhood first began with the relationship you had between you and a man, a relationship that will not take care of itself, but will rather dwindle if neglected. And though the kids may whine and fuss in your absences, they'll adjust easily when you're consistent and they will be forever grateful that you persevered and continued to make the marriage and that relationship a priority.

When I'm 110, I will also be thinking about the relationship I had and continue to have with my kids, who also are my best friends. I'll remember the thousands of hours of great memories together, the thousands of hours of family nights we had every week and the great vacations we took together every year. And because I'm investing in them when they're young, they will continue to invest in me when I'm old. My kids will come visit me every week, not because they have to, but because they want to. They will honor me, not because the Bible tells them to, but because they love me and desire to spend time with me.

Many women live through the lives of their children; they get their value and their worth from being a mom.

**Learn To Value Things Appropriately**

That will be my life. What about yours? The secret to having this kind of life—a life of no regrets—is to learn to value and esteem things appropriately.

I'm sure we've all watched *The Price Is Right*, the TV game show hosted by Bob Barker. Whether you know it or not, you can learn a lot from Bob Barker. This is what Scot calls "the Bob Barker Principle of Life": On the show, what happens when you overvalue an item? You lose it! You lose that item, and everything else you've earned, too, even if you overvalue it by just one dollar.

The same goes for life. When you over-value an item, you risk losing it, and you can also lose all the things you undervalue. Everything in life has value. If you want to live a life of no regrets, you have to learn to value things correctly.

The mom who values her errands may actually over-value them. Or, maybe you are addicted and consumed by the latest chick show airing on TV. Now, I understand that part of making a home involves cleaning and running errands, shopping and preparing dinner, running the kids to their various practices and appointments, helping with homework and teaching things like manners and hygiene. All of these responsibilities have value; I take pride in having a clean home and clean kids. And it is equally important that moms have their outlet for relaxing, whether it be the newest TV show, or reading a good book, talking on the phone with a friend, or meeting that friend for coffee. But if you find yourself spending only a few moments with the kids and the rest of your time spent running frantically here and there, you have overvalued the need to keep the house clean and the errands caught up. Maybe you find you've overvalued your "alone" time, keeping up with your favorite cyber space addresses or newest shows, and, subsequently, have undervalued time with your kids. The day will then come when the kids are out of the house or don't want to hang out with Mom because now they have things to do that are more valuable than spending time with you, and you will have regrets.

Get this. If you value time with your kids when they're young, they will value time with you when you're old. But if you value time with other things when they're young, they will value time with other things when you grow old.

You see, under the Bob Barker Principle of Life (let's call it the BBPL), you find the time, money, and resources for those things that are valuable to you. Similarly, you will find excuses not to do those things that are less valuable.

If you don't learn to get your values in order, you will find yourself with regrets in the years to come.

It isn't just what you say that counts, either. Because I know we all say, "Hey, my family is important, and my husband is important." Don't look at what you say; look at what you do. That will tell you whether you're headed toward regrets in life.

You might say your family is valuable, but what you might do is spend a few minutes a night with your children, tucking them in and then go finish up with the tasks you haven't yet completed, or rush off to catch up with the latest gossip among your friends. Now, those things need to be done; need to be completed, minus the gossip part, but is it more valuable than your relationship with your family? If it is, you will end up with regrets in life. You'll end up wishing you had done things differently where your husband and kids were concerned.

No one on their deathbed says, "I wish I would have seen one more episode of *Desperate Housewives*." But she might say that she wishes she could hold her kids one more time, spend just one more day at Disneyland, or spend one more day at the beach with her family.

You might say your husband is valuable, but what you might do is tell him, "Sorry, Honey. I'm not in the mood right now. I've been cooking and cleaning, and running, and being… I promise later I will make the time to sit and give you some attention. I just don't have the time and energy right now." Yet you don't blink an eye when the phone rings and it's the same friend with the same problem wanting you to share the same solution you've already shared time and time again. Or find the energy to run to the mall to buy that pair of shoes you've had your eye and heart set on. These we have time for, but to offer our husbands what they need most in the moment becomes too much.

Keeping the house clean definitely has value. New shoes, the latest program, and friends have some value. But when they are more valuable than your husband, you will end up with regrets.

You might say, "Sorry, Honey, I don't have time to take a parenting class or go to the marriage seminar." Yet you have time to watch three hours of *American Idol*, run to Starbucks (forty minutes a day), talk on the phone (two hours a day, look at the bill it will surprise you), read *People* to find out what is going on with Britney Spears. Many women know more about what is going on in Britney's life than in their own children's lives. You can spend six hours scrapbooking a few memories with the kids, but only a few moments creating them. You take a scrap-booking class to help you be creative, but you can't take a marriage class to bring some creativeness to your marriage.

You can spend six hours scrapbooking a few memories with the kids, but only a few moments creating them.

You need to examine your own life. This may be your value system, but as soon as you revalue your life, it will change where you spend your time, money and resources.

Do you want to find out what is really valuable to you? This week, go through your checkbook and find out where you're spending your money. Then go through your schedule and find out where you're spending your time.

Let's look at a sample checkbook for a month's time and see where this family's values are. Is she living a life of no regrets?

- $800 for car payments
- $100 for 7,000 channels of cable
- $100 for high-speed Internet
- $300 for another new outfit
- $200 for new purse for the outfit
- $100 for payment on M/C for old outfits and purses
- $50 for the kids to go to Chuck E. Cheese pizza
- $40 for date night

Let's also look at a sample schedule for the week:

- 18 hours watching *Grey's Anatomy*, *Gilmore Girls*, *The OC*, *Smallville*… (The average women watch 2.5 hours a day.)
- 10 hours talking on telephone (The average women talks 1.5 hours a day, check your phone records.)
- 6 hours watching movies
- 3 hours lunch dates with friends
- 4 hours cleaning
- 6 hours on errands
- 2 hours doing laundry
- 5 hours complaining about how no ones helps out

- 3 hours taking naps
- 3.67 hours with kids (20 minutes a night and two hours on weekends)
- 1.5 hour date with husband
- 4 hours trying to get husband to talk, while he pretends to listen but isn't listening.
- 7 hours listening to music while driving
- 0 hours listening to self-improvement tapes
- 0 hours reading self-improvement books
- 3 hours reading newspaper
- 7 minutes sex with husband (Once a week for 4 weeks, I may have over exaggerated the time. Between 5-7 minutes a month—That right there is funny!)
- 20 minutes (exaggerated) of prayer
- 6 hours at the lake
- 1.5 hours of church (attending three times a month)

Is this life headed for regret? This person almost spends more time cleaning, running, talking on the phone, than with her husband or kids. She definitely spends more time griping and complaining about what's not done rather than looking to enjoy those things that are, rather than looking to the good that is in her husband and kids. Focusing on the gripes and complaints wastes many precious minutes and hours throughout the days and weeks because griping and complaining are negative actions that will in no way better her life. Instead, she could be spending time on things that could make life better—like reading books and listening to self-improvement tapes. She has to be in the car anyway, so why does she listen to the radio instead of a tape that will motivate and encourage her? At the end of life, what good did those thousands of hours of easy-listening radio do for her? They left her only regret.

Now I'm not saying you can't listen to the radio or watch *Desperate Housewives*, read up on latest tabloid news. They have value. We need to relax and enjoy life. But if those activities are over-valued, you will end up with regrets in your life.

Have I made my point clearly enough? Determine to live a life of no regrets!

---

[1]Chapin, Harry. Lyrics by Sandra Chapin. "Cat's in the Cradle." Verities & Balderdash. Electra, 1990.

# CHAPTER 7

## CREATING MEMORIES

It's is a pretty day out, and the family is taking a drive to Grandma and Grandpa's house. Off in the distance, we see a huge hot-air balloon getting ready to take off. It's exciting to see your children enjoying things for the first time. I turn around in my seat to see Laken, now three, light up with excitement and surprise. Laken, since the moment he could speak, has been impressing us with his extreme intelligence and ability to put thoughts together and express them in such an adult manner. But, out of nowhere, my child—who has been brought up in a Christian home where we have spent our lives pouring God's Word into him, instilling character into his little soul, and trying to train him up in the way that he should go—says in a slow dramatic voice, "W..H..A..T T..H..E HELL IS T..H..A..T?"

Immediately I'm thinking that maybe I heard wrong, so I ask, "Laken, what did you say?"

He then, for my benefit, says it a little slower so I can understand him: "What-the-hell-is-that?" I turn around in my seat, cast an incredulous look over at my husband and he says, "Where in the hell did he learn to talk like that?"

In order to live a life of no regrets, we must get our values in order. Right values will mean we live a life of no regrets.

First, make sure that people are valuable to you. Of course, your husband and kids will be the most valuable to you.

You know your values are messed up if you "lose it" when someone accidentally spills coffee on your new Coach purse, because that inanimate object—your coveted purse—is more valuable to you than people. You have to wonder about your value system if you allow your kids to talk back to you or your husband, or allow them to treat either one of you like garbage—but heaven forbid if someone touched your scrapbook area. When your kids backtalk you or their father, you're forgiving and only mildly concerned, but when your prized new shoes are found in the mouth of the dog, you're ablaze with passion, ready to discipline all those involved!

One way to start getting your values in order is to take on the responsibility of creating memories in the home. Let's walk through some suggestions of practical things we can do. Let's start with the bare minimum. We covered some of this in the last chapter, but I want to encourage you again.

Starting this week, figure out what night is going to be family night, and let all of those who should be participating (children and Dad), know that under no circumstances is anyone exempt from this practice. A tradition, that from this day forward will take place, regardless of whatever else is thrown your way!

Growing up in our house, we had a family night, and my mom made sure nothing—I mean, no emergency, no friends, no relatives—ever messed with our family night! It was protected by her iron will! As a kid, that made me feel that family time was important to Mom; something highly valued. We meant more to her than anybody or anything. It created a sense of unity and an attitude of togetherness. Once a week, we knew for sure we were going to work on our relationship as a family—only, it wasn't work; it was great fun. Be encouraged, if you're not already doing this, if this is going to be something new for you and your family, it is a process that takes time for everyone to embrace. Make no allowances for absence, but know that it takes time to become a habit.

~ In order to live a life of no regrets, we must get our values in order. ~

And you know what? Family night didn't mean we went out to a restaurant or spent a lot of money. We didn't have a lot of money growing up. My parents were house-parents for a children's home, so family night usually consisted of playing a game together or maybe an ice cream run. We played all kinds of games: Uno, Scrabble, Monopoly, Life, Family Feud, Trivial Pursuit, War (the never-ending game), Nertz (our family favorite),

Hearts, Crazy Eights, Old Maid, Go Fish, 500, Hangman, marbles, memory games, charades, and so forth.

Some nights we would take a late night swim in the pool, or show off our newly learned skills on our bikes: "Look, Mom and Dad, no hands!" We would watch movies, have a picnic dinner at the park or barbeque. We LOVED drive-in movies (these are better than regular movies, because you get to have more talking and relationship time), we would take a drive to one of the nearby lakes and go fishing. We loved dressing my younger brother up like a girl in my Girl Scout uniform, and then perform a play for my parents. We also enjoyed just taking walks, or sitting and hearing our parents re-tell stories about each of us as babies, or stories from when they were younger and growing up with their parents and siblings.

I remember my dad would get out a pair of boxing gloves and teach us the correct way to punch and jab. It was really important to him that his son and daughters knew how to stand up for themselves and protect ourselves. It usually ended up with us acting goofy and rolling around on the ground. We would go shoot BB guns at a nearby shooting range, or take our ATC's out riding in the desert. My mom would often get us involved in baking cookies, or making ice cream floats…and so continues the list. Are you getting some ideas now?

I have so many vivid memories of our family nights, they were worth remembering. And now this is what I want my children to have. Like me, I want them to be able to fill up a book with memories of "family night." (Even as I write this, I can't help but smile as memories pass through my thoughts. I can't help but say what a great childhood I had thanks to my mom and dad making family night a priority in our week.)

So schedule it! Don't just say, "This week, we will have family night some night." It won't happen until you schedule it for a particular night. And you will not believe how excited your children will get about this. When Baylor was just three years old, he had no clue about the days of the week or of time in general, but come Wednesday morning, he knew: "Mom, family night is tonight, right?"

Schedule it and then fight for it. Make sure, if at all possible, that nothing gets in the way of family night.

Another practical thing you can do to change your values and create memories in the home is to make sure the family takes a family vacation. Now this is something you have to plan, schedule, and make sure happens every single year. It may sometimes be tempting to think money is too tight but you could use that same excuse every year until the kids are grown and out of the house.

Vacations are times when you get away from all the problems and stresses of life for a minimum of five days and focus primarily on each other, on relationships and on memories. You can't put a price tag on that. What's amazing is that you can do this for a very reasonable amount of money.

As I said, we had very little money growing up, but my mom made sure to push Dad to schedule a vacation every year. He would say, "Let's just stay home," or, "What about next year?" No! We will have a vacation every year; make it happen!

Every year we did something. Maybe it was going to the beach in California and staying in a cheap hotel. Sometimes it was camping out at the lake. Disneyland was possible if we scrimped on the hotel accommodations.

Our vacations growing up were never about the money spent or even about the places, but it was always about the relationships. Our mom made sure we had a vacation every single year. She made sure that she and Dad put away $10 a week (that was one fast-food trip we didn't take, videos we didn't rent, or popcorn we skipped at the movies). At the end of the year, we had about $500 for a vacation.

If you make it a priority, you will find the money.

Maybe you're thinking to yourself, we will just vacation at home and spend time together there.

But you won't. You'll do housework, call friends, and deal with all the everyday demands of life. No, you have to get away from everything and focus on each other to create a warm, lasting memory in the hearts of your children.

A week away is the minimum requirement to build those strong family memories, but I suggest you also do at least two mini vacations a year. Try to take a couple of days every year camping, skiing or boating. You have Spring Break and Winter Break—use these times wisely. Be creative and remember that the most important thing you can do is make memories for your kids. When your kids are out of school, your attitude has to be, what can I do with this time to produce a great family memory?

A week away is the minimum requirement to build those strong family memories.

On that same note, we have to get the mindset that weekends belong to the kids. That is another time to create a memory. I realize we need our husbands to do work on and around the house and the weekends are a great time for gathering the children to clean our and organize spaces that are cluttered, like closets and bedrooms. But try getting those things out of the way first as a family and then spend a few hours together. My family gets up on Saturday mornings. We eat breakfast together, and then we all clean the house and work in the yard together as a family.

I realize that this won't be one of your kids' most fun memories, but it puts in their hearts the importance of unity and of giving back to the family. The reward is that you then get to do something together, whether it's a picnic, a swim day or a pizza night.

Of course, when your kids get older, you have soccer games, baseball games, gymnastics events, piano recitals to attend—you name it. But it's important that even at these games, you go together and participate as a family. The idea is that, "You go, you watch and support your brother, and he will do the same for you." We always make it fun and exciting with snacks and treats, but find we are training them to enjoy time with each other as well.

What was hard for my husband to adjust to was that before we had kids, Sundays for us were church and sports day. He loves—and I mean loves—football! When football season is over, a part of him seems to dim inside, and that part doesn't come alive again until the next season in September. For him, trading football time for time playing t-ball in the backyard was hard at first, especially since he works for a church. He doesn't get home from church until about 1:00 p.m., and has to be back at 4:00 p.m. to preach.

But I refuse to lose a whole afternoon to something as meaningless as football. And I expressed that to him, sharing with him the importance of placing his family first. He is such a resourceful man, and began taping the games and watching them Sunday night after the kids are in bed and while I am off having some of my much needed personal time and space. Sunday afternoon is all about them and us as a family. And you know what? We have found that when we used to have that Sunday nap, we were actually more tired at church that night than when we forced ourselves to go out and play with the kids. After a couple of hours outside, we found we were more energized and awake; ready to conquer the Sunday night service!

You see, I know the time will come when the kids are grown up and out of the house. I hope and pray that because we invested and gave up things and time spent doing other activities along the way, like Sunday naps and football games, that they will still spend Sundays with us, coming over with our grandchildren and having "Mom" time.

Think about it—what could possibly be better than spending time with your kids? Friends come and go, but family is forever. Sure, we need time with friends and even getaways with friends. But that time should never replace the time we spend with our kids. I fight hard to make sure that every week, we get as much time as possible creating memories together; creating as a family.

Next on the list for creating memories is to make sure that holidays are special. Never let a holiday go by without celebrating it together. A great holiday celebration creates powerful memories for your children. There are so many great things you can teach your children concerning giving, particularly during the Christmas season—how good it feels when you give, why we give and how to receive. Be sure to make Christmas special. Get the tree together if you pick out a live one each year, plan a night for family decorating, put up lights on the house or plan a night to go out looking at lights; maybe bake cookies or make Christmas cards! Make that time of year special for the family.

While we're talking about Christmas, let me remind you that presents are never an option; you and your husband should always get them for the family. "Well, this year we're just going to give to the poor," you tell your family. But come on! "For you have the poor with you always…" (I borrowed that from Jesus in Matthew 26:11), and your family is your priority.

Now I'm not saying that we shouldn't do something special for the needy. It's important for your children to recognize they are blessed! In our family, we take our kids out and have each of them pick out a special toy for a needy child. We even let them help pay for it out of their own money. This is something we have been doing for a long time now, a tradition we started early on, and one that they take great pleasure in contributing to. They get so excited about this particular event that we actually use it as one of our family night activities during the holiday season. But, this desire didn't just "happen" inside of me. My mom, too, felt very strongly about the heart of giving at Christmas.

> This desire didn't just "happen" inside of me. My mom, too, felt strongly about the heart of giving at Christmas.

Growing up, my mom would set up a table in the family room. Sitting on this table would be everything we would need to make our own wrapping paper. She would set out markers, crayons, colored pencils, stencils (cookie cutters work great too), stickers, glue and the biggest roll of white butcher paper I had ever seen. She would include bowls of nuts, candies, and a tray of various types of cookies. This table was put up right after Thanksgiving, and remained until December 20th. On the weekends, she would have us go through our closets and toys and pick out gently used items that she would wrap using our homemade "wrapping paper." She would then contact the nurses' offices of the local elementary schools, and would arrange to drop it off, to be given out to families that needed extra help during the holiday season. My heart soars at this remembrance. What it taught me as a child is still being carried with me today in my adulthood. It is so important to teach our children to give outside of the family, but we should never sacrifice giving to the family in order to do it. If you do, there is a good chance your children will grow up resenting giving to the poor.

In our family, we make sure that each child has something special under the tree. (And of course I make sure my husband has something from me that says, "Dad is the best, and this is to say thank you for all you do.") Now, your kids' presents don't have to be expensive gifts; it's not about money, but about sacrifice and thought put into it.

Please enjoy the following story written by my husband which I never tire of hearing: "I received a garbage can, of all things, one Christmas when I was a child! It was a Green Bay Packers garbage can to be exact. And while it may sound stupid or cheap, I know my dad had to put away some extra money for that. But he knew how much I loved Green Bay. It came nowhere near the cost of my friend's $300 bike, but I guarantee it meant more to me than his gift did to him.

"It would have been easy for my dad to say, 'We have no money for gifts this year.'

"And because I love him, I would have happily said, 'Okay, Dad.' But my dad bought an amazing memory for just $12."

You see, moms, the gift doesn't have to be great, but it does have to be special and maybe even involve sacrifice of some sort. It should say, "I know this about you." (Scot's dad knew how much he LOVED the Green Bay Packers as a child, and that is why a simple trash can could mean so much.)

To me, Christmas was an amazing time of family, of giving, and of receiving. It was a whole month of anticipation and love. Christmas is about memories, thanks to parents who never let one go by without making a special time of it.

Birthdays are the same way. I have heard families say, "Let's not make a big to-do about birthdays." Why not? It gives you an excuse to create a memory and to celebrate the day that God brought your child into your lives. A child's birthday is an awesome day and deserves to be celebrated. Make your kids feel like this is a huge day, and make them feel important—as if life would not be the same had they not entered your family. Once again, you don't have to give them expensive gifts, but they do need gifts. They need a cake and a day of celebration, of laughing and of being together with their family.

Of course, you need to make sure all the siblings buy something for the birthday boy or girl, too. Teach them the importance of giving to their siblings. Put that habit in their hearts, and it will continue the rest of their lives.

For the rest of the holidays, get crazy. Don't hesitate to make a tradition of some sort during each one. Do the Easter-egg hunt. As a grown-up, my husband actually did the egg hunt with his parents until we had kids. He was twenty-four years old, hunting for eggs at his parent's house! And even then, his parents made it fun with riddles and clues they had spent hours writing. My mom always buys my siblings and I something special for the holidays and likes to send us on scavenger hunts to find them. Plan the Memorial Day barbeque, the Fourth of July fireworks, the Labor Day trips. Change your attitude to seeing these days as opportunities to create memories with your family.

As your kids get older, allow them to help out with the planning of family night, holidays, and vacations. When they get to help in the planning, they are more excited about the doing.

Finally, plan to have a "date" at regular intervals with each child. I have four children, so I do something special with one of them each week. Our date isn't hours long. It may be just going and getting a Slushy or a Happy Meal. It may be a taking a walk or taking them along to the mall and letting them choose the place where we eat. I feel it is important to have that one-on-one time with each of your children when you really talk to him or her. Having a special outing with your children helps them open up and talk about the stuff going on in their lives and their thoughts about it. When they do finally open up, you want to really listen to them as you let them talk.

This is especially valuable concerning you moms with sons. They learn how to date and what to expect from women by watching you. They learn how to value a woman by being taught how to treat and value you. They learn how to communicate with a woman by conversing with you. If you fill that mother/son need, he will feel comfortable to ask questions when the interest in girls sets in. He will be less likely to seek and follow wrong advice from friends, quite possibly making fearing the opposite sex obsolete.

They learn how to value a woman by being taught how to treat and value you.

Also, I encourage you to get a family hobby. It might be camping, water skiing, snow biking, bike riding, hiking—the list of possibilities could go on and on. But whatever you choose, make it a family hobby that you can all do together. We recently bought "quads," or four-wheelers, and we take them up to the mountains once a month. It's something fun and different that we can all participate in together, even mom—a girl! Our city kids get a chance to go out into the woods and ride their quads, build forts, shoot BB guns, build campfires and so forth. It gives us an excuse to get together. We spent $10,000 on these quads, so I guarantee we will ride them this month! Our hobby, in a way, makes us make time for family, fun and memories.

Please put into action what has been shared in this chapter: Create memories with your children when they are young, and then you will experience what you desire—kids who still spend their holidays with you as you grow older and who still take one vacation a year together.

Maybe you don't have a lot of special memories of time spent with your own mom and family. Yes, your mom worked hard to provide a loving home environment, and you knew she loved you. She was there. But memories were never built. A relationship was never developed. I want to challenge you to break that cycle. That cycle of lacking in relationship can end with you. Look for memory-making opportunities, and, instead, in the final analysis, you will end your life with a big smile on your face. As your life flashes before your eyes, it will be filled with priceless images of time spent with your family.

If you're looking for great ideas to create memories of your own with fun family nights, creative vacation ideas or to post ideas of your own, go to:

www.DadMomBook.com.

# Chapter 8

## Liar Liar!

About a year ago, I was grocery shopping with my six year old, Baylor. We had just parked, and were walking in the entrance of the store when he asked if I would buy him a toy today. Now, this is a practice that had begun to be abused, for every time we went shopping I would allow the boys to pick out something small. Scot and I had recently decided that it wasn't training the boys to a very good habit. What it was teaching them was a lack of self-control. I had actually just discussed with him that even our reasoning in saying no needed to direct them back to self-control rather than lack. For example, instead of saying, "No, we're not going to buy that today. I don't have the money," we had begun to instruct them with "No, we are CHOOSING not to buy anything today." By using the word "choose," we feel we are directing them back to their ability to have self-control, regardless of financial status. Just because we have the money to buy something doesn't mean that we have to have it. Okay, so that has nothing to do with where I am headed in this chapter, however, it's good information, don't you think?

So, I had just explained to Baylor that we were not going to buy toys. We grabbed a cart and continued on our way. Several minutes passed, when out of nowhere he says, "Mom you're a liar. You are, Mom."

Now, I've already shared in an earlier chapter that I am rarely speechless, but this took me completely off guard. Baylor is, along with his dad, the funny guy in our family, but I was having serious trouble finding any humor in where this comment was heading. I pulled him and our cart down a deserted aisle and with a look that said, "Hey, I'm curious but not far from being irate," I responded, "What did you say?"

"You're a liar."

Knowing I was heading into a very "teachable" moment, I asked, "Why would you say that, Bay?"

He then began to explain to me that just a couple of days ago, he had done something extremely kind and helpful for his younger brother, Peyton. He continued, reminding me that I had told him that the next time we went shopping, I would buy him a toy of his choosing for having been so nice. As he was sharing his explanation, it all began to come to the surface.

Ever had that happen? Where something begins to sound vaguely familiar, and now you have that feeling of, "Uh Oh, Mom is the one getting the lesson?" This was beginning to look like one of those times for me.

After explaining, of course, that there is a much more acceptable and respectful way of reminding me, I apologized to Baylor. I didn't try to use any excuses, just flat out told him he was right, I was wrong; I was sorry. He got to pick out his toy that day, and I was reminded that trust can be so fragile.

In case you haven't figured it out, this chapter is about the importance of keeping your word, because it is such a foundation to trust. Keeping your word is the key element in building a trusting relationship. How can a child possibly trust a mom who doesn't keep her word? How can a child trust the advice of a mom who, over the years, has never been consistent with her promises?

Keeping your word is the key element in building a trusting relationship.

**Liar, Liar…**

A great homework assignment for you would be to watch the movie *Liar, Liar* as a visual illustration of what broken promises can do to the heart of a child. The movie is about a dad who makes promises to his son that he neither has the intention nor ability to keep. Though the movie is written from the point of view of the father/son relationship, moms don't have to use too much imagination to put themselves in the same scenario.

It's a great movie, but isn't it funny how we as adults can watch a movie and forget about any questionable things in it—things that, say, a six year-old shouldn't see? I'm speaking hypothetically, of course. But this brings me to another personal illustration of the detrimental effect a lie can have, something that took place on one of our family vacations.

Scot had set up for me a couple hours to go and enjoy the resort's spa. So I head in the direction of the most amazing massage ever while leaving him alone with the children. Earlier I had posed the question, "What are you and the kids going to do while I'm gone?" He had responded that he just wanted some "down time," and planned to put on a movie and lay down with the boys. They were going to relax and watch a movie together. The movie of choice on this vacation so far had been *Snow White*. We had watched it so many times on the way to California, and Scot was so sick of hearing the songs, that I knew he and the boys would probably fall asleep the moment it began. Little did I know which selection he had made as he cuddled up with our five- and six-year-old sons.

Upon returning to our room, I heard my family of men laughing so hard. I knew something was up, however, when I opened the door and saw Scot flying through the air to get to the TV.

"Whatcha guys watching?"

With huge, wide-eyed innocence, my husband replies, "Nothing. We were having a…Bible study?"

Uh huh. Sure.

Not too long after, Scot heads out the door to run to the store, and I inform the boys that I'm going to take a shower. They ask if they can watch one of their movies, which is a great idea, considering I kind of need them to all stay in one spot, without hurting one another or damaging anything, while I shower. I had just turned off the blow dryer when I hear my sons giggling hopelessly, and a phrase that I couldn't quite place, repeating over and over "…It's probably because you have big boobs. I want to box them, Ma-ma!"

Thinking, "Oh my gosh, they somehow accessed a porno channel!" I swing open the door to find them watching and laughing, with remote in hand, rewinding a scene from a movie I own; involving a woman very well endowed. As if that wasn't enough, both older boys began reciting to me the entire two-minute scene, including the part about "boxing them."

My reaction? "Your dad is in so much trouble!" Movie watching had just been removed from our vacation.

The ultimate point is that we don't want to be like the father in that movie, who says things but doesn't follow through. I want my children to realize that when Mom or Dad promises something, we will do all we can to make sure it happens. Part of the reason that's so important to me is that when they are in their teen years and I say something that contradicts what their friends are saying, I want them to hold true to my words. In their hearts, they will know Mom doesn't lie—that what Mom says always turns out to be true.

To build a trusting relationship, a mom must keep her word to her children.

I don't know if you realize it or not, but your children hold on to everything you say. So we'd better be careful with those statements we just throw out there, such as, "Hey, kids, this weekend, let's go to Chuck E. Cheese." Then when the weekend comes and goes, Mom once again filled the child's heart with an empty promise. Or Mom promises that she will watch her child's next soccer game, but then that child watches and sees Mom talking to all the other moms, not watching at all. Sure, she had an excuse; one particular mom always has to start a conversation with her. But to have an excuse is to admit you're wrong. Let's work at not needing an excuse at all.

**Disappointed by a teacher**

Your child makes a mental note of every broken promise. Think back to when you were a kid. You probably have some memory of a parent or an adult who made empty promises. You have memories of promises you held on to and were disappointed.

I remember looking up to a specific teacher in school. This teacher had noticed a passion in me and had commented that it was hers, too. She would tell me time and again about a couple of contests that she felt I should compete in; that I would do so well in them. Every time I would see her, she would spend extra time talking to me, suggesting that we should set aside some time to perfect what I so enjoyed. She would always end every conversation with the promise to send me to these competitions. I needed a teacher recommendation in order to take part and participate in these events.

~

To have an excuse is to admit you're wrong. Let's work at not needing an excuse at all.

~

It never happened. Again, every time we would talk she would go on and on about how much she enjoyed them when she was in school, and how she could just see me loving it, and doing it every year! And, yet, not once did she ever get it together; follow through on her promise. She would say, "I promise you I'm going to call for the paperwork!" She would claim that she had friends on the planning committee, that they too, would be so good for me to meet and talk with!

This went on for years, and yet, all it amounted to was talk. I remember walking away from one such conversation thinking, you are so full of it. You are the type of person who says one thing, but does another, offers the world and opportunities, but never follows through. It actually stopped being a compliment at some point, and started feeling more like a slap in the face, just a random comment thrown at me by a really good actress who possessed the ability to get you to believe her every time. Because, at one time, I had truly believed her, and somewhere had hung onto a hope that she would finally, one day, make it happen. It was more than disappointing; it was crushing. It made me wonder if she ever really had seen potential in me or if that, too, was a lie.

My goal in sharing my story is to show you how a simple broken promise—just one—can potentially destroy trust in a relationship. My teacher had started with good intentions, and I know in my heart that she wanted to make me feel good about myself. But the damage of her broken promises outweighed all the positives in her flattery and fun conversations.

I know how fun it is sometimes to excite the kids with, "Hey, this summer, let's go camping." And maybe at the moment, you really want and intend to go. But understand that your kids recorded what you said in their memory, and if summer comes and goes and you don't go camping, you just lost a good portion of your credibility with them.

"Well, why wouldn't my kids remind me of something I promised them?" you might ask. The question is, why should they have to? To me, it wasn't my place to say, "Miss Teacher, when are you going to meet with me and get my paperwork done?" She promised, and since she was the adult, I figured she would wait until the time was right for her.

I think the best thing a mom can get out of this chapter is to remain quiet when it comes to making promises to her kids unless she is sure she can fulfill the promises she makes. If you're not positive you can go camping this summer, don't say anything. Then when the time comes and you can go, it will be a pleasant surprise for the kids. If you're not sure you can go on a picnic this weekend, don't raise false expectations. Wait until Saturday morning, and if it works out, it will be an exciting surprise.

One of the most detrimental things you can do to your children is to build up false expectations. Think about your own life and how mad you get when your expectations aren't met.

For example, let's say you saw an ad advertising seventy-five percent off at the Mall. You get all excited and leave early in the morning to get there. When you enter the store the lady says, "I'm sorry. We canceled that sale." So after you made your one phone call down at the police station, you are reminded that no one likes to get their hopes up, and then feel lied to. No one likes false expectations. Had you just gone to the mall like you do every other day, if there was no sale, no big deal.

Look at it this way. Let's say all week your husband talks about the awesome weekend get away you will have this weekend. You go out and get some nice things. You pack. You tell your friends. Friday comes and goes; no weekend trip. Saturday comes and goes; no weekend trip. Once again you find yourself down at the police station for assault.

If the husband was smart, he wouldn't say anything if he was not sure you would go. If he could take you, then on Friday it would be a pleasant surprise.

You see, your word is so important. It raises people's expectations, and nobody gets their hopes up like children. So if you even think you won't be able to do a certain thing with your children, don't say that you will. If you do promise you'll do something with your children on Saturday, for example, then do everything possible to do something with them on Saturday. Make it happen. And if you tell your children that you're going camping this year, get it on the books and start making plans—protect it, and allow nothing to stand in the way of it happening! Remember, your children don't want your excuses; they want a trusting relationship with their mom. They want you to be a woman of your word and to back up with action the things that you say.

Your word means everything. In fact, the rest of this book will be worthless if your word is worthless. You will never develop a relationship with your children if they can't trust every word that comes out of your mouth.

Can you trust someone who never keeps her promises? How much faith would you have in a financial advisor who constantly lied to you? Would you give him control of your finances? No! Likewise, do you think your teenager will give you any control in his life if he can't trust what you say? No!

> How much faith would you have in a financial advisor who constantly lied to you?

You may think your children are too young to remember your broken promises. But children remember.

My son Laken was only three years old when I realized that even children of his young age know when you don't keep your word.

Scot brought home a video game one night at about his bedtime. So he said, "Tomorrow before bed, we will play this game." The next day he forgot. It was seven o'clock and it was bedtime. I remember Laken throwing a big fit about going to bed, which was very unusual. Although he didn't like going to bed and whined a little each night, it had been quite some time since he had actually thrown a fit about it. With a forceful voice, Scot said, "Knock it off and get into bed!"

As Scot was tucking him in, he could tell Laken was really troubled by something. After about twenty minutes of our asking what was wrong and his saying nothing, finally as we were leaving the room, he said, "Dad, are you going to play that game after I go to sleep?"

My heart dropped. Scot said, "No, Son, you and I will go play that game right now."

What if I had dismissed the whole situation as his being rebellious or overly tired or just spoiled and had sent him off to bed? We could have lost a little bit of his heart that night.

Keeping your word has to become a priority in your life. Am I saying you can never break your word? No, of course not. Things do happen. Maybe you had to run one child to a birthday party you'd forgotten about, causing you to miss the soccer game. Or it rained and you couldn't have the picnic you'd planned. But how are you characterized? Do your children trust in the fact that you will do everything possible to keep your word? At the moment of truth will they think, Mom missed a soccer game. Something big must have happened because I know that my mom does everything in her power to keep her word?

If that is the heart of your children, then if you do have to cancel something that you'd planned together, it doesn't bother them. Why? Because they trust your word.

Keeping your word needs to be a lifestyle. If your kids see you lie or break your promises to others—especially to the most important man in their lives, their dad—it constantly sticks in the back of their minds, I wonder if she would do that to me. Once again, broken promises bring judgment.

So let your yes be yes and your no be no. Anything more than that carries the potential of ripping away at the core and foundation of your relationships. Remember, building trust is the core of your relationship with your kids, and the key way to do that is to always keep your word to them.

# Chapter 9

## I'm Sorry—What Did You Say?

While driving along one day, Baylor, age four, suddenly asks me who the devil is. Now, he can't just ask something easy like, "How does our vehicle move?" He has to go straight to a deep, spiritual question.

I answered, "Well, yes, we believe the devil is real, but doesn't necessarily look like the devil you have probably seen drawn in cartoons and such. Rather the devil uses people to try to influence you to do wrong things, things you shouldn't do."

"Is he real?"

"Yes, we believe he's real."

"So, he likes to get me in trouble?"

"Yes, I believe that's true, too."

"Is the devil a liar?"

"Yes, you should never trust the devil."

Baylor thought for a minute and said, "You know what, Mom? I don't think I'm going to hang out with THAT guy."

Well, that was easy. I was very glad that I had given serious consideration to his young, but very important need to resolve that in his young mind. I was glad that I had stopped what I was doing, making it a point to listen to what my son was saying, showing him that his thoughts and what they mean to him were important to me.

Just the other night, I was trying to share with Scot about how his not listening to me was really becoming a problem. Ever had THAT conversation with your spouse? I'm standing there really sharing my heart and he has this look that says, "Blah, blah, blah, I'm not really paying attention to a word you're saying, but I think I'm really succeeding at pretending that I am."

I saw the light bulb POP on. He truly joined in the conversation, long enough to reply, "You're right, Hon. Communication is a vital part of any relationship." While nodding his head and saying, "That's right, Honey," a few more times, he drifted back to never land or golf land, or football land, while I began to write this chapter in my mind. Now, understand this came out of my heart for my husband and our relationship, but I am raising children who will one day find themselves in intimatae relationships. I want them to be able to offer those in their life what they need and desire. What better time to start than right now, when they listen and believe so much of what I have to say?

Communication isn't always about just what you say. It's also about what you do. It has been said that words only account for ten percent of what we communicate; our body language, tone, and actions account for the rest.

Like you, I want to communicate love, security, and trust to the hearts of my children. The right kind of communication is at the heart of trust. It is the "blood" that brings nourishment to the "body," or the relationship. In other words, if communication doesn't exist or isn't good communication, the relationship can't grow and function properly. Many relationships suffer "heart attacks," and sometimes they're fatal because Mom lacks some or all of the skills of communication.

The right kind of communication is at the heart of trust.

Now there are different ways of communicating in which we as moms must learn to develop or perfect. For example, there's the "problem-solving" side of mom that says, "Hey, we need to do this and that. Please go do it." Then there's the "discipline" side of mom that says, "Do this and that—or else!" While neither of these ways is wrong, necessarily, they are not the ways of communicating that I'm going to discuss in this chapter.

There is a way of communicating moms can easily miss; it is the communication that builds the relationship with their children. It is communication that allows each person to share those deep things inside, such as hopes, dreams, aspirations, and feelings. In this type of communication, we share a part of ourselves—who we really are—with one another.

The reason it's important and we need to learn this type of communication is we want to communicate love to our children. In communicating love, we provide a safe atmosphere that fosters trust. To communicate love is so much more than just saying the words. I read a great book once that said, "…faith without works is dead." In the same sense, words without actions are dead. We have all had relationships with people who've said, "I love you," but nothing in those people's actions lined up with their words.

You may have had a mom who could say she loved you, but growing up, you felt no love. The goal is for our kids to go out into the world every day and feel sure about their mom's love. I want my actions to line up with my words so that my love for them is never in question. My kids may question the love of those outside the family, but Mom's love is never in question.

Love is an action; it is something you do. So moms, if you're not already, let's do love.

**Communicating Love With Actions**

You may think your actions agree with the words you're communicating to your children but there's an aspect of putting action to words that I want you to consider. You may think you're loving someone with your actions, but whether you realize it or not, the person could be missing the significance of your actions, because those types of actions do not indicate or express the love they need, a love spoken to them in a specific and unique way. We all have what are called love languages, and love languages are how we give and receive love.

(This next section is a brief overview of Gary Chapman's book *The Five Love Languages*.[2] I strongly suggest you read this book. Reading it changed my life.)

Because a particular love language is how we receive love personally or individually, we tend to think everyone else receives love the same way. But in reality, that may not be true. So you may be doing all kinds of things for your husband, for example, and after a while, you starting feeling like, What the heck! He is the most unappreciative person I know!

At the same time, he is upset with you because, in his mind, you never show him love! In reality, it's not that you don't love him; it's that you aren't loving him the way he needs to be loved.

Let me give you an example of how this works in the parent/child relationship. A mom comes home and says, "Son, I bought you one of those new action figures you like to add to your collection. Why don't you open it and go play?" The mom who shows her love for others with gift-giving does so because that's how she best receives love. When someone gives something to her, she feels loved by that particular action. So to show love, she gives gifts. And she feels that her actions are indications of her love.

But suppose this mom's son, on the other hand, likes quality time. Having quality time with someone he loves makes him feel loved by that person. So the gift of the action figure doesn't mean as much to him. He would give anything in the world if Mom would take a walk with him and talk with him—or come play action figures with him!

If Mom doesn't recognize her children's "love languages," she will go through life feeling like she gave her kids the world but was never appreciated for the love she showed them. And the kids will grow up having never felt loved by their mom. Once again, it wasn't that mom wasn't giving love to her son; it just wasn't the right type of love.

Here's another example. Maybe a mom feels love best through spending quality time together. She says, "Hey, Son, let's go for a walk and get some ice cream." But her son never really wants to go. So the mom begins to feel like her son doesn't want to spend time with her and is rejecting his mother's love. In the meantime, the son, who is best loved by acts of service, feels rejected by Mom.

This son would love it if Mom helped him with his school project, help him build a fort, or help by being his baseball team's "team mom." When it doesn't happen, that boy may grow up feeling like Mom wasn't there for him, which is untrue. Mom was there—just not in the way the son needed her to be.

Many moms get frustrated because their kids act and may even verbalize that their mom doesn't love them. If you identify with this feeling, understand that it may be that you're not loving them in the way they need it most. In other words, you're not communicating your love in the most effective way for them.

What good is giving something to someone else if it is something he or she doesn't really need? If we're going to communicate love effectively, we need to find out what our loved ones need and then give it to them. As moms, we need to learn the languages of love and find out what each of our children's primary love languages is. Then we can make sure we are communicating love to them through those languages—through those ways of communicating love.

What good is giving something to someone else if it is somethng he or she doesn't really need?

**The Five Languages of Love**

There are five primary love languages, and here is a brief overview. (But, please, get the book. It is more comprehensive, and if you want to be really good at something, you need to fully understand it.)

**The Giving of Gifts**

Love language number one is what I call the "show-me-the-money" or the gift-giving language. There are those who feel most loved by receiving gifts. These are the people who get really excited to find money in the card rather than eloquent words that suggest the person took great amounts of time in choosing what to say and write.

Now, to "speak" this language to your kids, you don't have to buy huge, expensive gifts. You could just get them something that says, "Today I thought of you." Right now, in my nine-year-old's life, this is his main love language. It's not that all kids don't want gifts, but to some kids, gifts tend to be a little more special. I can come home with gifts for all my kids, but Laken carries his gift around for days. He shows everyone what Mom got him. Heath, my eight year-old, plays with his gift for ten minutes, and then off he goes. He's very thankful for the gift, but the gift itself doesn't communicate love to him like it does to Laken.

**Acts of Service**

Love language number two is what my husband calls "What have you done for me lately?" or "acts of service." This love language is communicated when you do something unexpected or outside the norm for someone. For example, if my husband comes home and I have taken out the garbage for him, I have communicated love by doing an act of service. Because he is an acts-of-service person, that really says I love him. He feels I did something for him that I knew he would appreciate, and that makes him feel loved.

For your kids, this particular love language of acts of service may be communicated by fixing their bike, building a tree house, dressing Barbie or, in their teen years, helping them work on their car or teaching them to apply makeup and do their hair.

As I said, my husband is an acts-of-service guy, so this love language comes naturally to him. Not so much to me. And maybe not so much to you, either. Maybe you're a gift giver, so instead of helping your husband or children fix something (an act of service), you miss it by offering, "I'll find someone I can pay to help you out with that." The mom feels like she's showing love to them, but if their love language is acts of service, the mom is missing an opportunity to love her husband and child effectively.

**Quality Time**

Love language number three is quality time. Some people love to just sit and talk and share life. Quality time requires that you give yourself to the conversation; you listen closely and give the appropriate responses. Realize that time is a factor in showing love through spending quality time, but you must also realize that you don't need three hours at a time to show love to someone who is best loved by quality time spent together. You may spend only ten or twenty minutes, but to that person, those few minutes made his or her whole day.

A child whose primary love language is quality time needs time each day when Mom listens to him tell about his day. A ten-minute walk, sitting out on the swing or letting him ride with you to the store may be all you need to do. So if your love language is acts of service and your child's is quality time, you could make her favorite dinner, but she will think, Thanks, Mom, but I would rather that you just talked to me. I can make this myself, but I can't have a conversation with my mom without you.

**Words of Encouragement**

Love language number four is words of encouragement. For some kids, you can say, "You are so good at that," and it lights up their countenance, while other kids just say, "I know." If your daughter's "language" is words of encouragement, or affirmation, you could tell her, "That dress really looks amazing on you," and that one little phrase will fill her "love tank" for the whole day.

This love language is simple to communicate. Just look for areas in which to encourage your kids. You don't want to flatter them, but you do want to find sincere ways to say, "You're great at that."

I believe Heath, my eight-year-old, is motivated by this love language. When I say, "Son, you are so good at gymnastics! You're a natural," he gets this half smile on his face and gives me an embarrassed little nod. But then he walks away with a skip in his step. On the other hand, I can tell Laken, "You are very good at baseball," and he looks at me and says, "I know, Mom."

> A ten-minute walk, sitting out on the swing or letting him ride with you to the store may be all you need to do.

**Showing Affection**

The last language of love is physical touch and closeness or affection. To some people, a big hug, a hand on the shoulder or an arm around them during a movie fills them right up with love. A person who's motivated by touch also loves just to spend time with someone she loves. What makes this different from quality time is that you don't have to talk to communicate love. You can just be around each other. So you could be doing the dishes while your son is doing homework nearby. You're not having some deep conversation; you're just near each other. This time spent together means the world to this child.

If physical touch and closeness describes your child's love language, plan time when you can just be near him or her and give this child the extra hugs he or she needs.

As you read this, you might be thinking, My kids have all these love languages. They want the gifts, the service, the time, the words, and the touch—they want it all! In some sense, this is true. You have to realize that your kids' true love language won't really emerge until they're about eight years old. Your kids need to be loved in all these ways, but your job as a parent is to find the one or two ways that are especially meaningful to them. So study these languages, knowing that your kids possess a need for each one, but one or two will be the most important to them as they get older.

Now, it's important that our children are taught and learn to recognize the differences in showing love. We don't want to instill or foster a type of selfishness that always has them looking to see if we, as moms, are using their love language all the time. It's important that we require they exercise the use of the same knowledge when loving us back. This information should be used as tool in relationships. When children are also aware of the different love languages, they can better see and know when mom is operating out of hers.

**Conflict Resolution: Understanding Our Differences**

After you understand the five languages of love, you can see why so many fights and arguments happen in relationships over the years.

I, for example, am a quality time person, with a secondary language of physical touch and closeness. My husband was genuinely surprised when he found that physical touch wasn't sex. He has tried many times to add love language number six—sex, imparting to me that this is all men's primary love language. Actually, his love language is acts of service and gift giving. So, if I buy him something and keep the house clean—man, does he feel loved!

Before we read the love language book, a typical night consisted of the following. He would come home from work at least once a week with some sort of gift for me, and I would say, "That's nice. Thank you," and then put it away. That annoyed him so much. I would then follow him throughout the house, talking to him while he cleaned up, put things away and fixed things—until I was raging mad at the fact that he wasn't listening or considering a word I had said! At which point he would get mad right back, claiming me to be rude and unappreciative of the gift he had just given to me.

Then on the weekends, I would want to do what he thought were some of the dumbest things ever. "Hey," I'd say, "why don't we drive to Payson?" (Payson is a town about a two-hour drive away.) When he would ask why, I'd say, "I don't know. Let's just have lunch up there."

He would, of course, respond, "No, let's just drive right up the street, have lunch, and come home, clean the house, and wash some white t-shirts." He's very particular about having clean white undershirts. You see, I wanted that closeness of just sitting and talking in the car all the way. In his opinion, that's what his version of what hell would be—just one long drive...

When you understand and begin to communicate these love languages, they will change your life. You'll understand your husband's language, your kids' languages, your friends' language, mom, sister, kids' teachers, etc.

We need to use these love languages to communicate effectively with our kids and with those closest to us. Learn how to nourish those relationships with their life-blood—communication.

Learning to communicate correctly teaches your children the love and security they need to have a healthy, trusting relationship with you. Remember, communication isn't always just about the words you say; it's about your actions, too. When you begin to understand your children's love languages, then you can truly communicate love to them, which, after all, one of the highest goals of being a great mom!

---

[2]Chapman, Gary, *The Five Love Languages: How to Express Heartfelt Commitment to Your Mate*, Chicago: Northfield Publishing, 1995.

# Chapter 10

## I Still Can't Hear You

Our son, Heath, is a gymnast, and every year, like any sport, he has his competitive season; a series of months where he competes at various invitationals against other gymnasts. It was at one such event when he was about nine years old where I received yet another lesson in learning to listen. I had just sat for two hours watching him attempt and successfully complete what I would have to deem the hardest of skills.

To really appreciate the story, you must know that this is a sport that required not only the dedication and commitment on our son's part, but on ours as well. At this time he was putting in three hours a day, three days a week at the gym, which calculates to lots of money and time being spent. The sacrifices he made were great. He often missed out on Friday nights (one of his practice days), had to make sure homework was the first thing completed when he got home from school (practice was literally right after he got home), and spent those practice times doing heavy conditioning and weight training.

Yes, a lot for a nine-year-old little boy. But, a sport for which he had an amazing drive and passion. We had "happened" upon his natural talent in this sport when enrolling him and his two other brothers in recreational gymnastics at the local gym. Within three weeks, the recreational coach had made his gifting known to the gym's competitive coach, and Heath was invited to join the team and begin his career in competitive gymnastics.

From day one, he surprised us all by catching up quickly to the other gymnasts and began competing within the next seven months. Being fully apprised of what this sport was expecting and requiring of him, Heath agreed, and from that day on, has been setting personal goals and records and has yet to complain about the hours spent practicing or the rigors and expectations of this sport he has certainly claimed is his "strength."

So, here I am, awaiting his routine on the pommel horse, a bench-like contraption that has two handles by which Heath is to rotate and swing his legs over and around. I have to add that Heath is short and while he is very strong, the lack of long legs makes this particular event difficult, and one of his least favorite to perform.

Heath salutes the judge and proceeds to execute the routine. But, something about the routine, and the fact that I have watched it more than several times, seemed off. It looked as if he had left parts of the routine out. Upon finishing, I see his coach pull him into a huddle and begin to instruct Heath using his hands and fingers to represent what he had just watched Heath perform. My assumption was that he was showing Heath the correct movement, further affirming what I had already thought—part of the routine had been forgotten and left out. This fact was readily confirmed by the electronic scoreboard showing in neon a very low score for his routine on the pommel horse. Heath went on to take first place in parallel bars, and first place on the rings at this competition.

"I don't know what the score was. We're not supposed to pay attention to them."

I had just made my way to the performance floor to retrieve my son, who was standing with his other team mates, talking and rummaging through the competition goody bag. As we said and goodbye and walked away, I asked Heath what had happened on his pommel horse routine.

Heath became very confused, shook his head and looked at me as if I had just grown a second nose. "What do you mean?"

"Well, I mean, what happened to you on the pommel horse routine?"

"Nothing."

"Nothing? It sort of looked like you forgot a part of the routine, and your score came up really low."

He paused, then looked at me, and very patiently, yet firmly informed me, "I don't know what the score was. We're not supposed to pay attention to them. My coach doesn't care about the scores. All he cares about is good gymnastics. And I exercise good gymnastics. My contribution is to the team right now, not to myself. Scores do not matter."

Ummmm. I mean, how does an adult respond to this lesson being so clearly taught by the child? I mean, my first thought was, "Sure, your coach has the luxury of not being concerned about scores. He's not spending the fortune it costs to let you 'dabble' in 'good gymnastics.'" But, stopping to assess what he had just shared, choosing to think before I spoke, I realized that my child was being coached by a person who was training my child to look at what mattered.

Questioning Heath further, I learned the coach had been training and teaching my son  that it wasn't the "stunts" he could do, or the scores that they gained him, but rather that it was the manner in which he performed those skills he was learning that were important. Heath shared that his coach was obsessed with doing things safely, and that through all of the hours of muscle conditioning and weight training, he was teaching this team of gymnasts not only how to perform the routines, but to do so with poise and grace. To think what I would have missed had I failed to listen—a line of thought that could quite possibly be helping to grow a true gymnastic champion.

**Be Quick To Hear, Slow To Speak, and Slow To Anger**

In the last chapter, I talked about the languages of love and about ways to communicate with your children that will convey love and build trust in your relationship. The next step in communicating with your children is to realize that they want to be heard. Therefore, we have to learn how to be great listeners. We need to be that person they know they can come talk to about whatever is going on in their lives.

Sitting down and sharing with Mom is an experience like no other. And as moms, this is what we want for our children. We want them to think, Mom seems to know what to say and when to say it. She guides me lovingly when I need it, and she just listens lovingly when I need it. She demonstrates a heart of compassion for even the little things in my life that are big to me. Going to Mom isn't something I do only when I have nowhere else to turn. Instead, it's something I love to do whenever I get the chance.

A really great book once imparted, "So then, my beloved brethren, let every man be swift to hear, slow to speak, slow to wrath."

We must be swift to hear or always ready to hear what our children want to say. To encourage this kind of mentality in our kids, we have to become masters at listening. Listening is a skill that we have to practice. It is about learning how to hear our children's hearts, rather than just the words that come out of their mouths. It is about learning to be sensitive to the situation, knowing what to say, how to say, and when to say something. And more importantly, it's about knowing when to say nothing. You cannot be a great mom until you learn to be a great listener.

We are to be slow to speak, meaning we are to think out in our minds what we're about to say. We don't just blurt out whatever pops into our heads. Here's why: "Even a fool is thought wise if he keeps silent, and discerning if he holds his tongue."

Even a foolish mom can sound wise to her children if she keeps silent. Yes, we want to speak into their lives, but it only takes one time of opening up your mouth too quickly to sound foolish.

We can all identify with being guilty of speaking too quickly at times. My son Laken, like his dad, is vertically challenged. In other words, they are quite possibly the handsomest men on the planet; but God compensated for that by making them the smallest—otherwise they would steal all the women from the rest of you. Because of his height, my husband knows what it feels like to be made fun of in the third grade. So when Laken told us about this kid at school who was making fun of his height, passion rose up inside his dad. It just so happened that this kid could have stood to lose a couple of pounds, which was all the ammunition my husband needed.

Scot, being the mature dad he is, who has written his own book on being a great father, and unbeknownst to me, asked my son a real character-building question: "Isn't that the big fat kid?"

Laken answered, "Yes."

"Son," he said, "it's easy to fix this problem. Every time he opens his mouth to you, call him fatty. Tell him to go eat a donut. Ask him how he can fit through the door, or how a chair can hold his big butt."

I'm not asking that you agree that this was an amazing piece of advice. Scot, after the fact, wanted to argue that it was God-inspired.

Everything seemed fine, and the problem seemed to have been resolved until Laken decided to share with me, Mom, about his dad's "inspired" idea. For reasons every mom can agree with, I didn't find it to be such a helpful, intelligent, or character building solution to the problem. So the two of us came up with a better plan, one that applied some character, in our quest to resolve the problem.

You see, in advising Laken, Scot had allowed some of his own junk to creep in—all because he didn't fully think it through before he spoke it out. He wasn't slow to speak.

We can all identify with being guilty of speaking too quickly at times.

My mom always used to say "Be slow to anger." There will be times when your kids come to you with a problem. And it makes you so mad that they got themselves into that situation. But because you want to keep them coming back, you practice being slow to anger.

Your mindset has to be, how can I convey a solution and get my children on the right path without damaging their trust? For your kids to come to you with a problem at all is trust. But if coming to you means facing a huge negative consequence, such as a yelling session, or you nagging them, then the next time, they won't come to you at all. You just lost the opportunity to speak into their lives.

Be quick to hear, slow to speak, and slow to anger.

**Characteristics of a Bad Listener**

We know it's important to listen to our kids, but we don't always know how to develop those listening skills. Sometimes it helps to know what bad habits we need to avoid before we can learn good habits. So let me give you some characteristics of a bad listener in order to show you by contrast how to be a good listener. We all possess at least one of these negative traits. Identify yours, and you will know what you need to work on.

**The Comparers**

The first characteristic of a bad listener is comparing. If you're a comparer, while someone is talking to you, you will compare yourself to them. Maybe you'll compare that person's hardships with yours. It's like the mom who says, "Son, I know you think your life is hard, but when I was a kid, I walked ten miles to school…in the snow…uphill…both ways…barefoot! So what I'm saying to you is, 'Be happy.' Your life isn't that hard."

Think about it. If you have a problem, you don't like to think that your problem is less important than the person's you're talking to. It's as if that person is saying, "Your problem is not big enough for me to listen to." And you don't want your child to feel that way, either—to walk away thinking, If my problem isn't important to my mom, am I important?

My father-in-law, whom Scot brags about constantly, did this exact thing one time in all of his thirty-four years of life. And though this doesn't necessarily pertain to me, it's a great story to illustrate what we are talking about, so, I asked permission to use it and share it. What stands out in my mind is that my husband wasn't a child when this story took place. He was an adult, but it still made him so mad! How much more impact or affect does it have on a child?

Scot had just had knee surgery, one of the big replacement surgeries. He was at home recovering and had gotten up to go to the bathroom, not realizing the effect the pressure of the pooling blood and his weight would have on the recovering knee. By the time he had hobbled to the bathroom, he was in a cold sweat from head to toe, and the pain just kept getting worse and worse until he had me really concerned. He hobbled back to the couch, where he laid, for several minutes wanting to scream out in pain. He began popping pain pills like Chiclets, but complained they were useless, not working.

So, I called his mom and dad, and asked them if someone could come over and be with Scot while I went to go pick up a stronger prescription. Returning from the store, I walked in to find Scot where I had left him, lying on the couch, close to tears from the worst pain he had ever experienced in his life. In his drugged-up state of pain and madness, he claims to remember his father looking at him and saying, "Son, you haven't had pain until you've had a kidney stone. They say the only pain comparable to a kidney stone is childbirth." At which point he accuses me of stepping in to agree with his dad, by saying, "Yes, your knee pain is nothing compared to childbirth." Later he admitted that if he could have reached his crutches, he would have attacked us both.

The point is, don't ever discount the emotional needs of your child by exaggerating your own pains in hopes of lessening his or hers. It doesn't work, and it communicates a lack of concern. Sometimes it's appropriate to share stories of your past hurts and pains that are similar to theirs. Growing up, when a boy broke my heart, it was comforting to hear stories of how my mom had walked through similar hurts, and to know and see that in time, she had gotten beyond it okay and without scars.

Don't ever discount the emotional needs of your child by exaggerating your own pains in hopes of lessening his or hers.

**The Pretenders**

I shared about the comparers. What about the pretend listener? That is the next characteristic of a bad listener. I can't tell you how many times I have been at the house, just doing busy work, making sure the kids are doing what they need to be doing. All the while my husband is doing the same, only to have him seek me out and try to exercise my love language, quality time, right at the exact moment I have sat down to continue reading a really good book.

Seriously, I could be at home for hours, completely available for him to get the urge to try practicing my love language, when at the precise moment that I am finally going to take the opportunity for some alone and quiet time, he wants to launch into talking about my deepest desires and feelings. I aspire to have these great sitting and talking moments with my husband. After all, it is my love language! But, in that moment I'm thinking, Why now? Why couldn't we have had this conversation sometime in the last two hours? I now have to either close my book, or look up periodically and pretend to listen to him, nod my head, and say things like, "Yep," or, "That's good," or " I totally agree," all while trying to process what has just happened to the characters in my book.

And then at the end of the conversation, he asks, "What would you do?" Well, since I didn't hear one single word he said, I have to say, "Honey, I think you handled it right."

"But I didn't do anything yet!" he proclaims.

"Oh! I must have misunderstood what you said," I fumbled.

"No, you didn't misunderstand. You weren't listening to a word I said!"

As moms, we have to learn to continue focusing on a conversation. And it can be challenging. Sure we may be women, who are multitasking wizards, but let's be honest and real. Sometimes the multitasking can become our focus and cause us to miss out on other, equally important matters or concerns. Or, in our attempt to have some "down time," we can convey to those around us that we are unreachable or not interested.

My kids actually prey on this weakness of mine. If I'm at the computer writing, they know that Mom is an easy target. It's so weird—in the back of my mind I can hear them ask a question. I can remember answering the question, but the answer to the question doesn't register for about fifteen minutes. And my answer rarely is about what is best for the kids; it usually is about what is quietest for Mom.

Scot comes in one day and says, "Why are the kids playing in the sprinklers out back? It's freezing outside."

I look up and, sure enough, it's the middle of February and the kids are one, running through the sprinklers, and, two, naked. I go outside, and I'm mad. "What in the world are you doing running through the sprinklers?" I shout.

"But, Mom, you said we could!"

"No, I didn't…uh, wait a minute."

And in the very back of my mind, I remember something or someone coming into the house and asking something about running through the sprinklers. And I remember thinking, It will get them out of the house for a bit, give them a bit of exercise and it will allow for me to write in quiet a little bit longer. To this day I would promise you what I said was, "Sure, but don't get your clothes wet."

On another occasion, I was watching an episode from a particular drama I like to watch. The kids were all in bed, lights were out, dad was downstairs playing video games, and it was "Mom time." I was so engrossed in my show, was completely taken in by the romance, not quite paying attention to the graphic scene unfolding until I heard someone giggle. I immediately snapped out my love trance and looked over to see my seven-year-old son sitting on the couch, struggling to hide a goofy grin.

"Why aren't you in bed?"

Laken stuttered: "Mo…mmm, you said I could sit and finish my homework."

I started to say, "No, I would never let you sit here while I'm watching my show."

And then in the back of my mind, I remember a little voice saying, "I still need to finish my spelling sentences."

And, now remember responding with, "Okay, you can finish writing them, but then you need to get into bed."

It was at this point that I realized I needed to be a better listener, that when someone asks me a question, I need to stop whatever I'm doing, direct and focus my attention on them and what they have to say.

Remember, the point of listening is to strengthen the relationship, so if you aren't really listening—if you're daydreaming, thinking about something else, or just trying to get the kids out of your hair—you're missing one of the few moments you will get in your life to really invest in your kids.

There will come a day when the kids are grown and out of the house, and those times they want to really talk will be fewer. Try to grab every opportunity you have to communicate to them that Mom is here, Mom cares, and that what they have to say is the most important thing in your life at that moment. There will be many more dramas, good books to read, many more times to talk with friends on the phone, and a lot more time in my life to write. But if I miss this moment with my child, it will be gone forever.

Try to grab every opportunity you have to communicate to them that Mom is here.

**The Mind-Readers**

What about mind-readers? These are the people who try to figure out what you're going to say and then finish your thought before you get a chance to say it yourself. I sometimes have thoughts of just slapping a person who does this and saying, "Didn't see that coming, did you?"

A good listener does just that—he listens. When you do the mind-reading thing, it's like you're trying to rush the conversation along as if you have other things to do that are more important. When you do this, you can't really give your child the attention needed to hear his heart. You are so busy trying to figure out what he is going to say that you miss what he is saying.

A great old proverb reads: "He who answers before listening—that is his folly and his shame."

**The 'Rehearsers'**

Another characteristic of bad listening is rehearsing, or coming up with a response while the other person is still speaking. How can you hear him or her if you're focused on what you're about to say next? Let the person finish his or her thought, and then take a moment to think about how to respond.

One of the biggest problems with "rehearsers" is that once they have formulated their response, they want to cut you off or hurry you through what you have to say so they can talk. My husband used to do this very thing. When he's around a group of people, he will interrupt my story with funny, sarcastic comments, then tease me about how long my stories are. This gift of his costs him dearly, for it causes me to retreat once we are alone, rather than put on that pretty lingerie he so loves to see me wear! In a heated argument about this, he said it was his way of making my stories interesting! As if they needed his help OR assistance! (Slow to speak, Scot, slow…to… speak!) Rather than listening to you, "rehearsers" will have you listening to them.

**The Wanderers**

Then there are those who filter conversation, meaning they examine what you're saying to see only how it affects them. Once they realize it is safe—that you're not saying anything that interests them—they let their minds wander.

So maybe you're a filter listener. Maybe you listen to your son talk about school, and you notice, There's no big problem here. He's doing well in school. So you let your mind wander and start thinking about what it wants to think about. Then as your child continues to talk, you start wondering, for example, what you are going to fix for dinner, or how you forgot to return a friend's phone call. Off your mind goes, making mental notes here and there, never hearing the whole conversation; you filter through only those things that matter to you.

**The Dreamers**

What about dreamers? This is the listening trait of those people who "drift off" while you talk. Come on, each one of us has at least one person in our life who has this characteristic. You know, you're talking and all of sudden their eyes seem to gloss over, and you know that they can't possibly be giving your conversation that reaction, because it's just not good enough to warrant the now goofy, dream like smile they are suddenly wearing. Or, they begin to nod and agree with you in all the wrong parts of the conversation? I love to say the most outrageous things until they snap out of it and join you in reality.

For example, I'd say, "Yeah, so there I was, naked, drunk and dancing and singing!"

All of a sudden, they say, "Naked? Why were you naked and drunk?"

To be a good listener, you have to focus your mind on what your children are saying and not let your mind wander.

**The Advisors**

What about the great advisor? This is the type of listener who is the mighty solver of all problems. Their view in life is, "Bring your problems to me and I will solve them." If you're this type, after listening to a few sentences, you turn your attention from what is being said to solving the problem and coming up with advice. But in the meantime, you miss everything the other person has to say. This was one of traits I had to overcome. I want so desperately for those around me to enjoy this life they are living. I didn't realize that it was causing me to give unsolicited advice, ways they could overcome the dilemma in which they were finding themselves. My heart was to help, but, it was rarely what the person was needing or looking for. They just wanted someone to validate them by listening to what they had to share.

Realize that every time your children come to you to talk, it doesn't mean they want advice. Sometimes they want you just to listen to their problems. It's annoying to have a problem you just want and need to talk out, only to find that the person you've chosen to talk to just wants to blurt out all the solutions you already know or the ones that worked for them, when all you wanted was someone to simply employ compassion and just give you the freedom to "unload."

To be a good listener, a mom has to be sensitive to that and learn to be quiet and wait for her kids to say, "Mom, what do you think I should do?" You will find that most of the time, when you wait, they will ask. But if you offer or force advice, they will probably resent it. No one likes unsolicited advice.

You will find that most of the time, when you wait, they will ask.

**The Know-It-Alls**

The next type of bad listener is the person who always has to be right. Nothing is more annoying than someone like that. This person may twist facts and even make up stuff in order to be right. If this is a problem with you, you first have to understand that you're human—you do make mistakes and you do not know everything.

Listen to your children, knowing that you don't have all the answers—and that your children don't expect you to have all the answers. Most of the time, they just want Mom to be there and to allow them to share.

Let me give you an example. I had been dating a guy in high school for a very long time, had invested many Friday nights, weekends and holidays into spending time with him, only to find during my first year of college that he was bored with the relationship and wanted to have fun, date other people. The intelligent side of me was saying, "Fine, go ahead, I'm the one away at college, meeting new people every day, loser!" But, the human side of me was hurting and feeling tremendous rejection and pain. I remember calling my mom and asking her why I couldn't be the one he wanted and when would the pain go away? My mom didn't have an answer, and didn't pretend to be making one up. She just made herself available to listen to what I was feeling, and let me know that she was only a phone call away if I needed her again.

Sometimes that is all we can give our children—some hope, some time with Mom, and a big dose of encouragement. And do you know what? That was enough for me fifteen years ago, and I'm sure it will be enough for my children.

**The Contenders**

Have you ever tried to talk to an argumentative person? Their views and philosophies of life seem to change like the wind. It's like they look for ways to argue with you. One minute they are saying something you completely agree with, but once you verbalize agreement, they do a complete 360 and begin preparing a defense for the opposite opinion! If you say the sky is blue, they'll say it's red and then feel they must prove you wrong. They interrupt your story, either to argue facts or to tell you what you said or did wrong.

I once had a friend like this. I remember one Christmas Eve, she had just gotten laid off from her job and was really disturbed by it. I said, "That really stinks! What kind of company lays people off on Christmas Eve?" (That seemed like the right response to me.)

My friend responded by saying, "Hey, the company has to do what it has to do. Besides, you don't run a company that size, so how can you judge what they do?"

Ummm. Okay. Be laid off, I guess, and do it without my empathy?

My point is, do you find yourself arguing with your kids all the time? It's simply not a helpful listening technique. Remember, you can't change them until you change you. No one likes to argue, and if your kids know that every time they go talk to Mom, they end up arguing, it won't be long before they stop going to Mom. Once again, we need to practice being swift to hear, slow to speak, and slow to anger.

# Chapter 12

## It Wouldn't Be an Argument If You'd Just Let Me Be Right

This is one of my favorite stories of Scot and Laken: Laken, at the ripe old age of five, made an interesting career choice. On the news one afternoon as he and his dad were headed out the door, they heard, "Tonight on 'Live at Five,' you will hear about the girl who stripped for a cop."

Laken asked, "Dad, why did the lady strip for the cop?"

Without thinking he responded with, "She wanted the cop not to give her a ticket."

"Why would the cop not give her a ticket?"

Once again without thinking Scot blurted out, "Well, Son, because then she would be naked, and some guys like to see girls naked."

"Why?" he asked.

Actually, that was a good question. Why? Scot wondered. But then it struck him, they were headed down the dreaded and greatly feared path of the sex talk. He said he kept thinking, "Dear Lord, I'm not prepared for this 'birds and bees' talk. He's too young. I still don't even fully understand the birds and the bees. I surely don't want to give him the same talk my dad did, talking about fallopian tubes and ovaries—which was obviously his ploy to confuse me in a desperate attempt to keep me away from it all."

"Well, Laken," he said, trying hard not to pass out at this point, "guys like…uh…guys have…uh," and then he said he thought of an example that he felt was from God. Without thinking it through, he asked Laken a question, "Well, why do you like to play with your Batman?"

I knew right then, as Scot was relaying the story that he hadn't thought that through enough. He said, howbeit too late, "Never mind that example." But very quickly, Laken asked, "Does the cop like to play with her?"

"No, Laken. Well, maybe—but that's another subject. God made man to…when he gets married..."

"Are they married?" he interrupted.

"No, son, they're not! I wish they were, but they're not." Then he just said it: "God just made us men to like to see girls naked. Get in the van!"

Laken seemed to accept this, was momentarily pacified, and Scot began to think he was out of the woods, but as they were driving, he heard him say, "Dad?" He ignored him, hoping he would leave him alone.

"DAD!"

"DAD!"

"DAD!"

"DAD!"

"What, what, what, what, Laken?"

"Do you like to see Mommy naked?"

(Scot claims it was at this moment that he lost consciousness for a while.) He replied to Laken, "Well, yeah, Dad enjoys a peak every once in awhile."

Then came the ever evil question: "Why?"

"Uhhhh…" Long uncomfortable pause…

"Is it because of her boobies?" he offered.

Scot began to pray; saying his mind was racing, as he had at that moment begun to break out into a cold sweat. Finally, he says, "Sure, Laken, Dad likes her boobies."

"Dad, when do I get to see girls naked?"

Scot very quickly commanded, "Son, not for a long, long time—not until you are married, which won't be for a long time."

Again, the dreaded question: "Why?"

"Well, Son," he replied, "because you have to grow up. And besides, Dad wants you to live with him for awhile, because when you get married, you have to get your own house."

Laken exclaimed, "Daaaaad! Come on! I don't have money for a house."

~

Then I just said it: "God just made us to like to see girls naked. Get in the van!"

~

At this he says, "You have to get a job."

Laken replied, "I don't want to get a job."

At this point Scot begins thinking, "Great, I'm raising a lazy pervert." This made him mad, so he blurted out, "You have to have a job to get money! And you're going to get a job!"

"Dad, I think I'll just use your money."

"No, Son. I promise you, you will get a job. You will work hard at this job!" says Scot.

"Dad what if I just use Uncle Ryan's money? He's rich."

"No, no, no. You will get a job, and you will earn your own money. You won't be a freeloader, not in my house!"

"What will I do, Dad?"

Ah-ha! That was one of those training moments that moms and dads so enjoy. Highly trained parents look for these moments because it is a time in which we can instill wisdom and biblical principles into the hearts of our children.

"Laken," he said with excitement laced in his voice, "you can do whatever you want to do, be whatever you want to be. Whatever you put your mind to, you can do. Son, what do you want to be when you grow up?"

Without any hesitation, Laken replied to his dad, "I want to be a cop!"

**Broken Relationships—The High Cost of Arguing**

We've been looking at what it takes to be a great listener by looking at some of the characteristics of a bad listener. In the last chapter, we left off talking about the "contenders," those who always want to argue. If your goal is building relationships instead of tearing them down, arguing is a useless tool for communicating. An old proverb says, "The wise woman builds her house but the foolish pulls it down with her hands." If you want to play the fool and tear down the relationships in your life, particularly those with your children, you are certainly free to do it. But why not build those relationships by doing things the right way?

In this chapter, we will explore the dangers of arguing and disputing with others.

When you argue, dispute, quarrel or fight—whatever you want to call it—you are getting into strife and opening your life up to a lot of negative results. When you argue ninety-nine percent of the time, nothing good comes out of it.

I recently sat under a speaker who posed a really good question. She said, "Why is it that we feel the need to let people know we already know something that they have just learned and are wanting to teach to us? Have you done this? Found out a really cool piece of information, like where you can find the best shoe sale? Gone as far as to share it with the friends in your life, only to have them shoot you down by saying, "Oh, yeah, I already knew that!" Ever have that happen? Or, how about that friend who wants to share their random piece of information that is completely false? And yet, telling them the real answer won't cause a cure for an illness. Rather it will just make them feel stupid. You know, telling them they're wrong just so you can be right? What, exactly does this prove, other than you may have a mean, vindictive streak? Sure, there will be times where you have really been told something else and maybe have been led to believe differently and are genuinely asking, "Really, I thought it was this…," a question you truly want answered. Otherwise, what does it hurt to let the other person be right? What does it prove? There are definitely going to be times when we are right, but, isn't just "knowing" you are right enough? Do we really have to point out that someone has been given and believes wrong information? At the sake of what? Being viewed as smarter? And what does that do to the other person speaking?

Understand this and life will be so much easier. The only way to win an argument is to avoid it. You cannot and will not ever truly win an argument.

You can't win an argument because even if you do win it, you still lose. Why? Well, let's say you win. You shoot your competitor's argument full of holes, and you prove that she is a moron and that you are the smartest woman on the earth. You walk away, leaving them feeling inferior and stupid. You have hurt someone's pride. They may resent your triumph. You won but you may not have changed anything. That other person might still think she's right. But now she's hurt, thinking of ways to get even and to prove you wrong.

Benjamin Franklin once said, "A man convinced against his will is of the same opinion still."

How many of us have been so right that we were dead right?

What is better—to win an argument with your spouse but have him pout all night and be mad—or to work out the disagreement in a way that everyone wins?

I read the following once in the *Boston Journal*. It said, in effect, "Here lies the body of Willey Jay, who died maintaining his right-of-way. He was right, dead right, as he sped along. But he's just as dead as if he were wrong."

How many of us have been so right that we were dead right? But now the relationship is dead, just as dead as if we were wrong. You may be right—you may be dead right as you speed along in your argument—but as far as changing another person's mind is concerned, you may end up with the same outcome as if you were wrong.

An old proverb says, in essence, that hate is never ended by more hate but by love. In other words, you will never win an argument, but you can love your way through a disagreement. Use this principle—just try it for one week. I guarantee you will then use it for life. It will take a majority of strife and anger out of your life.

Think about it. If you didn't fight or argue with anyone in your life, how much better would life be?

I was about twenty-five years old and I was shopping at the mall with a friend. We went into one of the department stores so I could purchase something I had placed on hold. We walked to the register where two clerks were busy chatting about their dates the night before. Being a fairly patient person, I waited a bit longer, before I finally said, "Excuse me, could you help me for a minute?"

It was at this point that both of the clerks decided to turn around and acknowledge our existence at their counter. "A minute? That's all you need is *a* minute? Rarely are customer questions resolved within the time frame of a minute."

Out of nowhere I replied, "Well, now that you have taken up more than two of mine, if you would like to close your mouth, I will wow you with my ability to pose a one minute question. You may then go and share the enormity of this feat with all your friends!"

Completely disbelieving that I, me, "sweet-put-up-with-rude-people-all-the-time-and-say-nothing-but-smile" me had just met sarcasm with better sarcasm, I braved a glance at my friend, to find her smiling triumphantly! Well, needless to say, the clerk was not impressed. I am no fool and recognized injured pride in the woman probably due to the snort my comment had received from clerk #2; a snort that clearly acknowledged I had won that round.

"I put something on hold here last night, and just wanted to purchase it," I quickly said.

With the best snotty smirk I have ever seen, she replies, "No, that's not possible. You see, we don't put things on hold." Now, what she wasn't privy to was that the item I had placed on hold was sitting in plain sight on the counter just behind her. I had already spotted it when we had first walked up, thus being the reason I knew I could pose the one-minute question. The other clerk was trying desperately to look busy while being able to hang around and eavesdrop; witness to just how far this episode was going to last.

"Oh, so the lady that helped last night isn't aware of your 'no holds' policy, then? Because, she distinctly and without issue took down my name, then placed the little hold paper on the hanger of the item," I said calmly; but probably a bit smug.

"No," replied she, "she must not be aware of the policy. Sorry."

Sure. I continued, "So, you have not seen a top with black stripes and a bow across the front? On hold for, Holly?"

"No," she replies.

The clerk listening in finally clues to the fact that I am staring directly at the item, clearly on hold, with the tag secured around the hanger, the tag that, in fact, does have my name on it. I think she probably picked up on this, due to the fact that as I posed my questions, I was staring pointedly at something just behind snotty clerk's view. I offered her a little conspiratorial smile; you know, the one that says, "Isn't she going to feel like a jerk?"

This banter went on for a couple of seconds longer, then I became bored and wanted to gain victory; truly wanted to buy my shirt and continue on our shopping quest. So, in my sweetest voice I gave her one last chance to surrender with a little bit of dignity, a chance for her to just do her job and look. "Are you absolutely positive you have not seen the shirt anywhere, and you can say without a doubt that no one would have placed an item on hold for me?"

She raised her eyebrows, smirked her smirkiest smirk yet, and slowly shook her head, no.

"Oh, okay," I say, "because, I am actually looking right at it."

At this point her clerk friend decides to step in and give her some assistance, but not before casting rude girl a glance that said, "You should have just listened to her one minute question."

Receiving my purchase, my friend and I turned to go, but not before I added, a bit too brightly, "Thanks. Enjoy your day!"

Ten years later I had a similar snotty experience with a sales clerk in yet another department store, but this time I just smiled and continued to be nice. When it came time to pay, I handed her one of our church business cards and told her I really hoped her day got a little better. The next Sunday, she came up to me in church and apologized. She was having a horrible day, problems at work and at home. She has been coming to church ever since.

Those are similar situations, but they had different endings. Why? Because although I can't control another person who's being argumentative, I can control myself. In the second situation, I took control of what I could control—myself!

> Although I can't control another person who's being argumentative, I can control myself.

If I could get Scot to just let me win all the arguments, life would be perfect. Learning the dangers of arguing will change the way your boss and your co-workers treat you. It will change your friendships and your relationships. It will change your marriage and your relationships with your children.

Remember, a misunderstanding is never ended by an argument—only by love. And where your children are concerned, your job is not to argue with them. Don't fight with them to get them to do the right thing. Instead, learn to guide and direct them with your love.

I'm especially talking about not arguing with your kids later, in the teen years. Sure, there may be times you have to say, "I'm not going to argue with you. This is the way it's going to be," because that is what's best for them. For example, you're not going to let your daughter at fifteen date the bum who's eight years older. She may be upset at first but I believe that when she calms down, then you can try to explain it to her. However, that doesn't mean the issue is open for negotiation. Sure, she may be upset, but in ten years, she will look back and say, "Thanks, Mom."

Scot at age fifteen, like most teenagers—knew it all. And he certainly believed he knew the right people to hang out with. There was this kid named Mike, who was one of those rebellious, cool types. He would want to ditch church and sit in the parking lot and chew tobacco. He even brought some Jack Daniels to church in a flask. He cussed, talked dirty, and was everything I guess Scot wanted in a friend. Scot's dad shared with me that he saw through this and said, "You're not allowed to hang out with him."

He said that Scot used every argument in the book, saying, "But, Dad, I could be a good influence on him. I could get him into church! Come on, what would Jesus do? Dad, I can get him saved."

All of these arguments, of course, were made-up excuses to get his way. The real truth was that he really wanted to hang out with this guy who was rebellious and "cool." But his father said, "No, and there will be no more arguments." The last Scot heard, this kid was in jail, serving a ten-year sentence.

My mom never argued with me. On big issues, there was no argument. It was, "This is what we will do." On little issues, she heard my heart and communicated direction and guidance to me.

Understand that argumentative "listeners" dabble in dangerous territory, allowing themselves to be tools of the devil. Arguing rarely wins anything worth having, but it does damage the people involved.

**Attributes of a Great Listener**

Now that we understand many of the characteristics of a bad listener and how to avoid these pitfalls when communicating with our children, let's focus on what it takes to be a great listener. This is the listener we should determine to be in all areas of life, but most importantly with our husband and children.

A great listener first wants to understand and then she wants to be understood. She recognizes that listening is an active process, not a passive one. In other words, she knows you have to work at it to be good at it.

A great listener is mentally alert to what the other person is saying. She realizes that we were given two ears and only one mouth for a reason—so we would spend more time listening than talking.

A mother who is a great listener generally does little talking but a lot of listening. A good listener sometimes plays ignorant, realizing that one of people's greatest needs is to feel important and to know things you don't know. A great listener at times acts like what her child is saying is something new and unknown to her: "Really, Son? I didn't know that. Tell me more." Come on, who doesn't like to talk when you feel like you're the smart one in the conversation!

A great listener shows genuine interest, stops what she's doing, and focuses on what the other person is saying. She concentrates on what is being said, not on what she wants to say next, knowing that you can't listen to yourself and to the other person at the same time.

A great listener doesn't jump to conclusions; instead, she lets the person paint the entire picture. A great listener motivates the other person to say more and uses verbal rewards that make him or her want to talk to her again. A mom who is a great listener might say, "Hon, that was an amazing story. You have a gift for telling great stories." This mom knows that any behavior she reinforces, her children are guaranteed to repeat, and she wants her children to talk to her.

A good listener uses what is called the silent pause. Nobody likes dead time or quiet gaps in the flow of the conversation, but a good listener tries to allow the other person to fill them. Oftentimes, that gets the wheels of conversation going again.

A great listener listens to what the person is trying to say, not just the words being said. She looks for nonverbal clues and tries to read between the lines. She takes out all the fluff and other junk and looks at what the person really is trying to convey—sometimes by what the person is not saying. A great listener listens with genuine compassion and puts herself in the other person's shoes. She tries to feel what the other person feels.

A great listener shows genuine interest, stops what she's doing, and focuses on what the other person is saying.

A great mom does all of these things, and she focuses on setting up situations to talk. Once a month, she takes her son out on a date when just mom and son go to dinner, and she lets him share his heart. A great mom takes her daughter on a walk, on a bike ride, or shopping. She looks for whatever activity she can come up with—it could be as simple as saying, "I'm going to put some gas in the car. Why don't you ride along?" She just carved out of twenty minutes of priceless conversation time with her child.

Becoming a great listener to your kids is simple. Remember, your goal isn't to talk, but to listen. And by showing them the importance of listening, you train your kids how to communicate in relationships in the future.

So become swift to hear, slow to speak, and slow to anger. In other words, become a master listener, someone your children will come to in order to share their hearts—now and for the rest of their lives.

# Chapter 13

## Your Child's Secret Place

Once when I was around ten years old, I remember volunteering to run errands with my mom. This surprised her because running errands with her had never been a huge hit with me before, especially if I could spend that time reading. I remember her asking me, "Are you sure you want to come along? It may take awhile."

"Yeah, I do," I answered. We then got in the car.

As she was starting the car, she said, "Maybe we should go grab some lunch first!"

We started talking about what she needed to pick up, and then the next thing I knew she was asking me if there was anything else we needed in the house that she had possibly forgotten to write down.

Finally, I worked up the courage to share, "Mom, I had a really bad dream last night. In this dream there was a witch chasing you down the street. The next thing I knew was that you and the witch were gone. When I woke up, I remember feeling good about the witch being gone, but in the dream, you never came back either."

I just remember her explaining to me that sometimes things happen in our day, maybe someone is mean, or unkind to us or our friends, and it sticks inside our mind; popping up as something scary and ugly in our dreams. Or, maybe there was some truth to my fear of losing her; thinking that she would go away and not come back or that she was too busy with others, and no longer had time for me.

At the time, we had recently moved to a children's home where my parents were "houseparents" to ten other children. The children's home consisted of five dormitories, four boys' dorms and one girls' dorm. My family lived in a dorm that housed ten junior high-aged boys. This had been a drastic change in mine and my sister and brother's lives, as we were now a family of fifteen, requiring more of my parents' time, as it was now being divided between thirteen of us rather than just the three of us biological siblings.

At that time in my life, I opened up a part of my heart that no one could get into without my permission. It was the first time I remember ever sharing a scary moment that still had me shaken up. I was a little scared because that area of my heart was so fragile, unsure of what I thought about my feelings and what I was dealing with. With my actions, I was saying, "Mom, come into my heart, and I hope I can trust you." Mom saw the opportunity, which could have been easily missed if she'd said a simple, "Why don't you let Mom run errands alone this time, okay?" But she saw the opportunity, came into my private world, and left my heart in better condition than it was before. It took a great deal of trust to open up this fragile place to her, and had she not treated it right, she would have broken my trust. And there would have been a great chance she would never have seen that part of my heart again.

For the next few years, there were countless more times I opened up that part of my heart to her. But here are a few of my more memorable ones.

Mom saw the opportunity, which could have been easily missed.

I was in the sixth grade, and I had just transferred to this school the year before; so, technically, was still the new girl. It was that time of year, time for the sixth grade play. This year the play was "Peter Pan." I so desperately wanted to play the part of Tinkerbell! I wanted it so badly, I could just see it! I was very tiny, just like Tink. And, I was blonde, also, just like Tink! I mean, it wasn't like I was asking to play the lead. Here I was still in some ways the new kid on the block, and all I wanted was just a supporting role!

But, as with many things in life, nothing is ever just that simple or that easy. My best friend wanted the same part. The day of auditions came and it went really well. I felt really good about my audition, and again could see myself in this role. But, inside I was still struggling.

I remember a couple of days before they were going to reveal the cast list. I had another heart to heart with my mom. She had just finished up in the laundry room, and I walked in. I began asking her very random questions about the new organizing set up she had just created. "So, how does each person know which cubby is theirs?"

She looked at me and smiled. A smile that said, "What's really on your mind, since I know you couldn't care less about the way I've just organized the laundry?"

In actuality, she did share about the organization, and did answer my question. As she was walking out, she said, "Follow me, and keep me company."

That was the only open window that I needed. "Mom, have you ever wanted something really badly that you hope inside that you get it, even though you know it would make someone else feel really good too?"

"Yes," she said. "I have felt that way."

"What did you do about it?" I asked.

"I hoped with every part of me, and prayed too," she said.

"Did you get it? The thing you hoped for?"

"No," she replied. "I didn't get it."

"Oh."

My mom wasn't done. "There are times in our lives where it's our turn to win. Maybe we studied harder, or maybe we are better suited for the thing we are desiring, but; then there will be those times when it isn't our turn, and we have to know to be okay—maybe disappointed, but okay."

I responded, "I just want this thing so badly, but I feel ugly, because in order to win, someone who's been really good and nice to me has to lose. And she wants it just as badly as I do. Am I an ugly person for not letting her have it instead?"

My mom had really good wisdom that day. I mean, she was right on. She went on to share that if I did drop out, she knew exactly WHAT it was I was wanting to "win," that who was to say that the teachers would automatically give the part to my friend? She introduced the point that I had been assuming that my friend and I were the only ones trying out for the part, but had I failed to notice if there were any other people who had also auditioned for the role as Tinkerbell? She really set me thinking that day, put my heart at ease and encouraged me that whoever got the part deserved it this time. And, no, I wasn't an ugly person for wanting something so badly.

Once again, I had opened up and said, "Mom, come into my heart. I'm still a little scared because it is fragile. But I trusted you before and I hope I can trust you again."

My mom saw the opportunity, which could have been easily missed with a simple hug and, "Don't be silly. Why would you think you're ugly? Go to sleep." But she saw the opportunity, my seeking something big, came into my private, inner world, and left my heart in better condition than it was before. It took a great deal of trust to open up this fragile place to her, and had she not treated it right, she would have broken my trust. There would have been a great chance she would never have seen that part of my heart again.

By the time I became a teenager, it got easier and easier to share that secret, fragile part of my heart. My mom had established in me that I could trust her. That she wasn't going to step in and affirm my fears, but, instead she took advantage of the opportunity to place something positive inside of me and left my heart in better condition than it was before. By this time I knew that if I could trust my mom with the innermost secrets of my heart, I could trust her with anything.

To build a trusting relationship with our children, we need to understand and respect our children's secret world.

**Our Three Worlds**

We all live in three worlds. We have our public world; that is where you spend most of your time with people—maybe those at work, church, or the fitness club. You know each other, but not very closely. You are friendly to one another—you may say hi and you may talk a little about surface things, like the weather, sports or church. But outside of small talk, those people don't really know you. That is the public world.

We also all have an individual world. The individual world involves family and close friends. In this realm, you share a little more about yourself and what is going on in your life. You share the little problems, the little concerns you have. You share the "surface" of your heart with these people.

Under the surface is a third world we live in. There, we have what we could call the "closet." You have some skeletons in that closet that you can't share with just anyone, or maybe there is no one you feel you can share these skeletons with. It's a place where you keep your personal thoughts, big wishes and hopeful dreams. In there lie the big concerns of life, things you don't like about yourself, your insecurities, fears and anxieties. It's where you store those memories you're embarrassed or feel guilty about. There are things in there you don't feel you can trust with just anyone. My question to you is this: Do your children trust you enough to let you into their closet?

You have some skeletons in that closet that you can't share with just anyone.

Your private, inner world is the most secret of all places. No one can visit your private world without an invitation. Therefore, you will never know what your children are thinking unless they let you into that world.

Your child has a private world that is constantly changing. Things that concerned you when you were sixteen are no longer part of that world by the time you're eighteen.

You see, what's in there is not as important as how we as parents treat the contents of that heart.

**Watch for the Open Window**

Moms need to be sensitive to this secret world. We need to know when our children are ready to open up that world. We should always be looking for it, because that window only opens for a moment. And if you miss it, that chance may be gone forever.

You see, the window isn't always open, and you can't open it on your own. Your child wants to open it, but needs you to want to come in. If you act busy, if you don't see it, the child goes away and closes that window. And that topic more than likely will never be available again.

I hope you are seeing the importance of this.

The window opens at the weirdest times. Maybe it opens when you're taking a walk or tucking your kids into bed. You could be doing laundry, scrapbooking, or watching TV. And it is almost always awkward. The child just comes and stands near you. He or she may help you do something that normally he or she doesn't do. Or she may want to go with you to the store or ride with you on an errand. What can happen is, if you don't know what to look for, you can easily miss that open window.

It would be easy to say, "Hey, why don't you go off and play? Let Mom work on this by herself," or "Mom has to do some quick errands by herself." But if you do—just like that—you missed it. You missed your child opening up the window of his heart and saying, "Mom, come on in. I want to give you a little glimpse of something that is on the inside, something in my private world. I'm taking a chance, Mom, because no one has access to this world unless I invite him. Can I trust you?"

I challenge you to look for this open window into your child's secret world. Anytime your child is hanging around, maybe even doing something awkward around you, pay attention. Do what my mother did. Stop what you're doing and give your son or daughter the opportunity to let you in. You will be building trust in them and in the relationship. If your children can trust you with what's going on inside, then they can trust you with everything else.

Since you want your kids to open up their hearts—and for the rest of their lives to keep opening up to you—you have to be very gentle and careful with what you do and say inside their secret world. If you condemn them, put them down or act like their concerns are no big deal, you might just close this window forever. Sure, you can still have a relationship with your child, but it will never be as close as the relationship that is allowed in the secret world.

Suppose your son comes to you and says, "Mom, I'm having trouble talking to girls," and you say, "Don't be silly! It's no big deal to talk to them. Why are you worried about it, anyway? You're too young to be thinking about that." You just went into that window like a bull in a china shop, knocking everything over, saying what he's feeling is stupid nonsense and a waste of your time. Your child will walk away, thinking, I love you, Mom, but I know I can't let you in here again.

Or maybe your daughter comes and tells you about her boyfriend pressuring her to engage in more than just kissing at the end of a date. What if you go off on her, telling her she can't see him anymore, because your family has rules and regulations—and punishment? Understand that had she not opened up to you, you would have never known, and the potential of finding herself in a compromising situation could have been much greater. You punished her for letting you into her secret world, and guess what? You won't be let in again.

Entering your child's secret world is like visiting someone's house. If you go in and trash the place, you won't be invited back. But if you go in, make sure you don't break anything, clean it up, and leave it better than when you got there, you can expect to be invited there again.

Please don't miss the window! Don't go into your children's inner world and condemn or punish them for opening it up. Instead, cherish every time and treat it like the treasure it is. Do this, and your children will be inviting you in for the rest of their lives.

Don't go into your children's inner world and condemn or punish them for opening it up.

I want moms of young children to understand that you want to be there when your little ones open that window and say, "Mom, come on in." For a little one of five, six or seven years old, their issues of life may not be very big to us, but they are major to them.

Teach your children early on that they can trust you with their innermost thoughts, questions and problems. To build a trusting relationship, we need to realize that there is another world going on inside that little life, and once in a while, that child is saying, "Mom, if I can trust you with my heart, I know I can trust you with anything." When children learn early that they can trust their moms with their secret world, then when they get into the teenage years, they will still say, "Mom, come on in."

Treat your children's secret world with respect so that you will always be welcomed back.

MOM

# Chapter 14

## Being the Source of Encouragement in Your House

I don't know about you, but I am not the same mom to my third and fourth children as I was with my first and second. I mean, I struggled with maintaining a level of perfection, standard and expectation that I just seemed to throw to the wind after our second son. I think we go into the whole idea of parenthood a bit idealistic, start adding more children to the grand scheme and realize, "I'll just be lucky if they all get through to high school knowing the importance of changing their underwear everyday!" I guess what I'm trying to say is so much goes into being a parent, being a mom.

And, we start out this destiny so eager and optimistic. We get into it, and find it's much harder than we ever could have imagined. We have emotions that need to be kept in check. We get a lot less sleep than we are used to (which only magnifies the need for our being able to control our emotions).

Suddenly, life really isn't about us, and then there is the whole time management thing. I haven't even begun the list, but don't feel as if I have to, considering that, if you're reading this, you are most likely a mom, know what I'm talking about, and would be depressed if I took your relaxed reading time to include list upon list of all of the things that moms do, which you could probably be doing now, rather than reading this awesome book.

I believe you get the picture. As you continue to add children to your home and family, you realize that some of your old ways of doing things would never work. They would require more time than you have to give, right? For example, when our first son was born, we boiled everything, every time! Seriously! He was not allowed a "binky" unless it had first been sterilized. We headed in the same direction with our second son, Heath, but became a little less rigid about it. You know, instead of sterilizing everything every time, we just had one big sterilizing party where we threw everything in, and if it didn't last through the week, then...well, at least we started off with good intentions.

By the time Baylor, our third son was born, we were throwing caution to the wind! Understand that I am exaggerating here, just a little, for the sake of making you smile. But Baylor, it seemed, became the guinea pig, the child that got the "relaxed and easygoing, not uptight" version of Mom and Dad. I think Laken and Heath knew their alphabet by the time they celebrated their first birthdays. We were just overjoyed that Baylor could walk by the time he celebrated his! Hey, he was certainly a happy baby!

We live in Arizona, so the number one thing to do during our very popular HOT summertime, is swim. I don't know the statistics, but let's just say everyone has a pool, or knows someone who does, because, unless you are playing in the pool, you are sitting in the house or somewhere that is air-conditioned. Yes, the stories are true, Arizona, during the summer is a scorcher! Carried in bulk, inside every Arizona Mom's swim bag, is sunscreen and bottled water.

It's the summer of 2003 and I am Mom to four little boys: Eight-year-old Laken, seven-year-old Heath, four-year-old Baylor, and baby Peyton who had just recently turned one. It was a hot summer day. The boys were out of school…we were heading to the pool.

I had just finished "lubing" up my kids with sunscreen, had reminded them to "walk, don't run" approximately ten times when I look up to see Baylor on the verge of hysteria. Getting ready to ask what was wrong, I remembered. He probably had just reached inside the bag to locate his "floaties," only to find that they had not been brought along on this particular Anderson swimming trip. Yep, this was the summer that Baylor learned to swim without them. And, one only had to look at his terrified expression to know that this was not a decision made by him. The older boys had learned to swim at a much earlier age, and by our estimation, Baylor was severely behind schedule!

One only had to look at his terrified expression to know that this was not a decision made by him.

To my defense, I started out very patient and encouraging. I placed the baby in the shade with his toys, then proceeded to get into the pool next to Baylor, who was sitting by the steps. After wading in myself, I extended my arms towards Baylor, who simply shook his head, no.

Now, I know I'm not the only person conscious of this, you know, the whole water pooling in the butt of your bathing suit every time you exit the water? Or the fact that getting out requires that we adjust our swimsuit; which initially gets too much air and balloons out around you? Well, I was in no mood to deal with the fashion end of swimming, which meant I wasn't going to exit the pool in order to force my child to get in. So, for the next fifteen minutes, I did that whole game where you pretend like it's so much fun standing in one spot swishing your hips around in an attempt to coax your child in through peer pressure, getting angrier by the minute because he's not buying it. "Ooh, come on, don't you want to get in? It's fun! Look, isn't Mommy having fun? (swish, swish) Don't you want to get in a cool off? Hey boys! Isn't Baylor missing out on all the fun (swish, swish)? Look Baylor, your brothers are having fun in the water! Come on!"

Finally, "Baylor! Baylor! Put your feet on the first step RIGHT NOW! Now! Let's go! Grab hold of my hands! NOW! Don't be a Baby!"

With every command, I grew more and more mad, more and more frustrated! I knew in my mind he was ready for this, would enjoy the pool so much more, and was absolutely determined to win this battle. It wasn't like this was the first time at the pool this summer, we had already played this game and had succeeded in getting him in the water for a couple of minutes only to cave in and put the "floaties" on.

Unfortunately, he was smart enough to know that couldn't happen today, because Mom hadn't even brought them. It was like his butt was cemented to the cool decking. I'm not proud of what happened next. The story has a purpose for continuing on in the chapter. I showed him what fun he was missing one last time (swish, swish), then became a completely different person.

Everything became blurry and red. I lost track of all sound going on around me, became really strong as I nearly RAN out of the pool and up the steps. Before I could even compute what I was doing, I had picked my son up, then… Up and over he went as I threw him in the pool. I know, you're horrified—think about how I was feeling! Something just came, took over my body and actions, and had just thrown my precious, cuddly Baylor in the water!

I hurried back in, wading toward him, only to stop just a foot in front of him as he dog paddled to the surface sputtering and gasping for air, reaching for anything nearby that could help him keep himself above water. Now, most moms would probably have realized the error of their ways, and would, by now, be reaching out their hand, helping their child to safety. Not me. I look back embarrassingly to what I did next.

"Come on, Bay. Come on, you can do it. Come on, Baylor, SWIM to Mommy!" Yes, ladies, right there I lost the mother of the year award. You can already imagine how long it actually took my son to get through his FEAR of the water, let alone learn to swim, after having been "thrown" that little lesson by Mom.

One of the biggest things we have to learn to communicate to our children is encouragement. Yes, there are going to be times where they will need a little push (not literally), to succeed at some things life throws them (Now I'm on a roll). But, we have to pay attention to the manner in which we are accomplishing this goal.

**We Must Contradict the Voices of Discouragement From the World**

We need to be a source of encouragement in our children's lives. Kids will receive enough discouragement from the world. They will be teased, made fun of, told they are "less than," or "not good enough," "not capable." The world will point out and focus on their little imperfections. We all have a few characteristics that by society's standards aren't normal, but being successful in knowing who you are comes by focusing on the great gifts and talents you do have.

As moms, it is our job to point our children to all the wonderful gifts and talents they possess. We should communicate this to them every day. We are the primary source of our children's self-confidence. We build it with the words, actions and beliefs we communicate to our children.

> As moms, it is our job to point our children to all the wonderful gifts and talents they possess.

What a tragedy it is when a mother is on the same level as the world, pointing out her child's weaknesses, with no solution on how to turn them into strengths, and tearing down a child's self-confidence rather than building it up. This mother puts her child at an emotional disadvantage and even handicaps him.

The Bible talks about the kind of person who does this: "It would be better for him if a millstone were hung around his neck and he were thrown into the sea, than that he should offend one of these little ones." I don't know what a millstone is, but I do know I don't want one hung around my neck as I'm being thrown into the sea!

Mothers should build their children up. They should be that voice inside them that says, "You can do anything you set your mind to, you are not less than, you are great looking, smart, fun, you have a great personality."

You see, when this belief system plants these truths in their hearts as children, they become adults who are still able to say, "I can do anything I set my mind to. I'm not less than. I'm great looking, smart, fun, and I have a great personality."

What voice do your children hear? Do your voice and actions communicate to them the truths of life or the lies of the world?

Take the time to point out the gifts and talents of your children. There is nothing wrong with telling your son he is handsome and that all the girls will be after him. And you make sure you let your little girl know she is a princess and that she is the most beautiful girl in the world. Try to say it in a way that's not just flattery, but that really speaks truth from your heart about the positive characteristics of your children.

Your children hear these words in the back of their heads when the world is talking to them. When the world says they're ugly and no one likes them, they know that Mom says they're attractive, have a great personality, and make people laugh. At that point, the trust level of the relationship kicks in, and the success of that relationship will determine whose words are true to them, their mom's or the world's.

I have to give you the perfect illustration of what I mean. Laken was four years old at the time and loved to play video games just like his dad. We had just bought the game "Crazy Taxi." It's a fun game in which you pick up pedestrians and then break every law known to man as you try to get them to their destination.

One day, as I was walking by the room where Laken was playing, I heard him yelling at the TV. I stopped and listened. He kept saying, "I don't suck. You suck."

I thought my son was hearing voices and, worst of all, talking to them. As I got closer, I heard a voice from the game say, "You suck—I'm outta' here!" and the guy in the cab jumps out of the car because Laken was taking too long.

Laken screamed, "I don't suck! You suck!" What made it funny was he honestly was mad that the game would say that to him.

Later in life, when the mean world says, in essence, "You suck," I want Laken, and all of my children, to still have that same confidence: "No, I don't suck. You suck." Even if all the world says he's a nobody, I want Mom's words speaking to him. I want all my kids to say, "My mom would never lie to me. I don't suck, and I'm not a nobody. I must be attractive, and I must have a great personality—because my mom says so!"

Do you see the power of your words in the lives of your children?

**You Create or Destroy Self-Esteem With Your Words**

As a mom, your job is to help your kids find the talents and gifts they possess inside. The great thing about this is that it takes just a few moments a day. It just takes a mom becoming aware of the power of words.

There are some things you can do. For one, make sure every day that you tell your child how awesome he or she is. Once again, it's not flattery, but if you look for it, the moment that's right for a true compliment will come up.

Laken came home from school one day and said, "Mom, I got a hundred on my spelling test."

I said, "Well, that hard work you did studying, and the fact that you're a genius, really paid off!"

There were two encouraging aspects to my statement. One, I pointed Laken to the truth that hard work does pay off. If you want something, you have to work for it. Two, on the tail end, I added a little extra to his heart: "You're a genius."

An old proverb says, "For as he (a person) thinks in his heart, so is he…" There's a principle here: As your daughter thinks she's pretty and has a great personality, what is within her, in her heart, produces something around her. She believes these things, and they become true.

It is an interesting phenomenon that if we hear something long enough, after a time, we will believe it. "How is my handsome boy doing?" you can say, or, "How did you get so smart?" Here are a few more: "How come you're so pretty?" "No wonder all the girls like you!" and, "I have the best children in the world."

I started saying these things to my children at birth. Over and over, I'm programming the message the "recorder" will play in their minds. You know that recorder I'm talking about, the one that tells you whether or not you can do something, the one that tells you if you're attractive and personable or not. It's that little recorder we call self-esteem.

~ Make sure every day that you tell your child how awesome he or she is. ~

Something I have always shied away from was telling my children that they are the "Best" at something. I have always tried to use, "You're one of the best at that." My reasoning for this is I don't want my children to walk in false pride. For one it's annoying, and secondly it sets the child up to fail through ignorance. You see, it's unrealistic to tell them that they are "the best," because reality is, there is always someone who is better. I want my children to grow up confident and striving, knowing that they are gifted and talented, but that doesn't have to be diminished by the fact that others are, too. I don't want to tell them they're the best, have them grow up to meet someone who may do better at what their attempting and be confused or now devastated that they are not the only person with a particular skill or ability. It's important and wise that I train them to be happy with their performance while recognizing and being able to congratulate someone else who came out even more ahead or further than they did.

And that reasoning is how this got started. You see, I personally can tell them that I think they are the best THEM, because, there isn't another one of THEM. The chances of Laken running into another exact replica of Laken are pretty close to nil. So, I started telling them, "You're my best Heath in the world!" "You're my best Peyton in the world!"

Again, being the best "them" in this phrase is referring to the fact that they are made one of a kind. It's different than a skill they possess, yet share with others who may, too, possess that same skill. This is personally pertaining to our own little family, our way of encouraging them in the fact that they are loved, capable and unique. And something they totally jumped on board with, making this phrase the way we say goodbye, goodnight, or even thank you in our house. Laken, Heath, and Baylor say, for example, "Bye, Mom and Dad. You're the best mom and dad in the world." Even our twenty-month-old tries, "Byeee mom ant dad urdbest intl wrd."

We answer, "Bye, Laken, you're the best Laken in the world. Bye, Heath, you're the best Heath…," and so on. What are we doing? We're programming their hearts, one, to look for the good in their parents, and, two, to see the good inside themselves.

If you look for the moment to encourage your kids, you will see it. But if you're not aware, you'll miss it. And then your children only get to hear what the world thinks and believes. And, sadly, that will then become what they think and believe.

**Elevate the Good in Your Children**

So tell your children how blessed you are to have kids like them. Look for areas in which you can express how proud you are of them. You know, in our society, we get so caught up in suppressing the bad in our kids that we miss elevating the good.

For example, you could say, "Son, I'm so proud of the way you treated your sister back there." You just elevated the good in him, and just to hear those words again, your son will look for an opportunity to make you proud. He'll start thinking, How can I do that for my sister again? You see, you didn't have to discipline him to treat her right; you just had to notice and encourage him when he treated her right.

The other day Baylor had "Grandma time." Now, time with Grandma consists of taking the grandkids out for ice cream, candy, treats and toys. I try to explain to my children that this is not the woman I grew up with. I tell them,

"You don't realize what we had to do just to get a Happy Meal." Needless to say, Grandma time is a real treat.

Well, after Grandma time, Baylor comes home with an awesome gift that he'd gotten for his birthday just three weeks before. I said, "Son, you already have one of these." He replied, "I know, Mom. But Laken wanted the one I got, so I got him one."

That right there was one of the truest acts of kindness I have ever seen. He gave up his toy to bless his brother. I hugged him and went around telling everyone what he'd done and how proud I was of him. The next day, we took him out and blessed him with another toy. I wanted to so elevate that good that he'd done that he keeps on doing it.

Think back in your own life to the times your mom said to you, "I'm so proud of you." It brings back a tingle inside of you, doesn't it? For those of you who never heard those words, what would you give to have heard your mother say that to you?

So look for areas to be proud of and then announce them to the world. It's one thing to say you're proud to your child, but it's another thing to tell those around you in front of your child. Doing that reinforces your belief in him.

Even as an adult, when my mom tells someone how proud she is of me, it makes my heart skip a beat. It puts a big smile on my face. If mom is proud of me, who cares what the world thinks!

We, as moms, should elevate the good, but how do we encourage children about their weaknesses? It depends on the weakness.

I think one of the greatest things that should be communicated to our children is that they have to power to change what they don't like in themselves, that we can ask God to help us change the things we have the power to change and to help us change our attitude toward the things we can't change. That is so wise, I'll say it again: We need to learn to change those things we have the power to change, and change our attitude toward those things we can't change.

~

One of the gtreatest things that should be communi-cated to our children is that they have the power to change what they don't like in themselves.

~

Teach your children this principle. Let me give you an example of how to do it. When Laken started baseball, like all parents, we thought he was going to be the best. Come to find out, because we waited until he was nine to get him in baseball, he was a little behind the curve.

On the way home from one particular practice, we pointed out the two good things he did and didn't mention the 100 mistakes. Every night after that, he and his dad worked on baseball for twenty minutes. The first three games, he struck out every time at bat. He would get frustrated, and say, "I'm no good!"

But in the Anderson house, those words are not allowed. "Son," I'd say, "you are very good. You are good at whatever you work at. We just need to practice some more this week. But remember that catch you made? That was great!"

"But, Mom, Dad," he insisted, "I struck out every time."

"Well, son, remember the last game we watched on TV? Sammy Sosa, one of the greatest hitters in the world, struck out every time!"

Laken and Scot started going to the batting cages three times a week. By the last four games, he only struck out once. And by the next season, he was the best batter on the team, hitting .650.

In Laken's weakness, we were able to encourage him and keep his spirits up and show him that Dad and Mom are proud of who he is, no matter what happens in life. We were able to show him the benefits of hard work—that if you're not good at something, it's easy to fix. You practice until you become good. This skill will follow him into adulthood. For example, if he were to find out he's not good at marriage, rather than quit, he'll know he can read books, get tapes and practice until he becomes good at marriage.

Now, in that account, did we once lie to Laken or give him false flattery? No, and let me tell you something. Kids can see right through that. If I had said, "Laken, you're the best baseball player in the world," he would have known that wasn't true. But we pointed him toward the good, helped him find the good, and then gave him the keys to becoming good.

You know, it's easy to become good at something when you have your mom backing you up.

**A Mother's Love Should Be Unconditional**

It is important that your kids get unconditional love from you. I love you not for what you do or don't do, but because you exist. Your children have to have this concept built into them in life. They have to know that no matter how many mistakes they make—whatever happens—your love is unconditional. There are no conditions attached. Your attitude is, "My love is for you, not for what you do. I'm proud of you no matter what."

For example, you might say to your child, "I don't like the fact that you got a D on your report card. But that doesn't change how I feel about you. I am still the most blessed mom in the world to have a child like you. Though I am proud of you, there will be some changes in your study habits and fun time until those grades come up. But my love for you isn't about what you do; it is because you exist. Though the world loves you for what you do for it, at home, you will always know that Mom's arms are open to you and that I'm here for you, no matter what."

You guide your kids into success by encouraging them toward the positive and showing them the benefits of hard work. They already know their weaknesses, so what they want is for you to notice their strengths and to be there to help them with their weaknesses.

I want to always be there to help my kids with their weaknesses. One time we were trying to show off Baylor, who was three years old at the time. Scot's uncle was visiting, and Scot proceeded to impress his uncle by having him (Baylor) recite his ABCs. So Baylor starts, "A B C D E F G H I J L M..."

I stopped him and said, "Baylor, you forgot the letter K. Start again."

"Sorry, Mom," he said and then, "A B C D E F G H I J L M..."

"Baylor," I said, "you forgot the K. It is G H I J K—K! Then L M and so on. So let's start at G."

"G H I J L...," he said again. I promise you, for one hour he could not get the K! Finally, he could do H I J K L..., so I said, "Let's start from the beginning."

Then he left out the G. I worked with him another twenty minutes to finally get the G back, but then he was missing the K again.

I am convinced that his brain could only hold twenty-five letters. For weeks, I worked with him, and I was close to not practicing anything I'm saying in this chapter. I got so frustrated, I wanted to just "go off." Finally, Scot and I came to the conclusion that the letter K wasn't all that important. We thought he could be quite successful without it. I mean Wal-Mart is just as good as K-Mart, and 7 Eleven is fine over Circle K.

A month afterward, I was working on numbers with Baylor, and, I promise you this is true, he could count to twenty but had no eleven. When we told my brother-in-law this story, he counted out the letters, and, wouldn't you know it, K is the eleventh letter! Scot joked, "I'll bet he has no November in his months of the year. And I guess there will be no eleventh day of Christmas. As an adult, a dozen eggs will be missing number eleven. And what in the world will happen at eleven o'clock!"

Of course, there will be things that your children can't change.

The point of this story is that, until Baylor got his K and the number eleven, we continued to praise him in the meantime in all that he did, and we focused on the twenty-five great letters he did know, not on the one he couldn't get. (But when you look at the chapters of this book, you will notice I left out the eleventh chapter. I did it for Baylor.)

Of course, there will be things that your children can't change. In these cases, you have to teach them to change their attitude toward it. My husband being just 5'5" learned this very fast. (And, it looks like my children will, too.) Growing up, he couldn't change his height, and his father couldn't change his height. And we all know that kids can be mean.

Actually, even adults can be funny about this, as if a person's stature is the only thing people feel the freedom to make fun of to your face. At least once a month, someone we don't know at the church will come up and say, "Man, you're short!"

That makes us laugh, because if we responded with, "Man, you're fat," or "Man, you're bald," "Boy, you have a huge nose," or "You are one ugly woman," that would devastate them.

Growing up, Scot could have been mad and thought, Why me? Poor me. Or he could be excited about who he was, what he has, and focus on all his gifts and talents. With his mom's direction, he chose the latter. He learned to laugh with people and to beat them to the punch on the short jokes. He focused on his awesome personality and good looks. He never allowed those things he couldn't change to attach themselves to his self-image. Today, he has a very high, healthy self-esteem.

Your children will have things about them that the world says is "less than." Some people deal with their own shortcomings by tearing you down to build themselves up. But we as mothers have the power to help build our kids' self-esteem so that it isn't ravaged or destroyed by the world.

I touched on this earlier but I want to emphasize that negative talk is not allowed in our house. "I'm stupid," "I'm no good," "I can't," "I'm ugly"—those phrases aren't allowed in our house, because those phrases, if said, will in time attach to my children's self-image.

If your child says, "I stink at math," you can say, "No, you're good at math, but we just need to practice some more on multiplication." Teach your children not to say what they feel they are, but instead to say what they want to become. In time, they can actually become what they believe, if their goals are reasonable and attainable, of course. If one of them feels horrible at math, he can say he is great at math. If he says it long enough, he will begin to believe it. Because he believes it, he will act like it, spending more time with the practice problems and hard work, and what he believes inside will produce the good result on the outside.

Another example is that your daughter may not feel beautiful. But she can say that she is. Before long, she believes it, and her inner beauty paired with this belief makes her treat herself like she's beautiful—maybe she'll start wearing makeup and dressing in attractive clothes or perhaps she'll style her hair—and she then becomes beautiful.

**Treat Your Children as Valuable and Precious and Ensure Their Success for Life**

How you feel about something determines how you treat it. If you feel like something is beautiful and precious, you treat it like it is. But if you think something is ugly and old, you treat it like that.

My first car was a 1964 Datsun. My parents bought it from my grandma, installed a stereo system in it, put a new paint job on it, slapped a bow on it and said, "Happy Birthday!" It was my sixteenth birthday present and I was thrilled! I had wheels! No more bus rides for me! I was so beside myself that I even named and purchased personalized plates! Its name was Tweety Bird.

Now, the stereo system was a bit flawed, didn't work in some areas; mostly the ones around where I lived and went to school and hung out, and the body of the car was a little dated. Did I mention it had belonged to my GRANDMA? It sounded a bit hollow when you closed the doors, and had the biggest dashboard I had ever seen. I look back and see that now, but then, what I saw was a car that was all mine and it was beautiful.

I kept it washed and cleaned out. It wasn't a BMW or a Mazda RX-7, but it belonged to me. It took me and my friends to lunch. It drove me to school. It enabled me to go out on the weekends without parent assistance. It was freedom and responsibility, and I loved it. I saw its value, treated it as valuable and it became valuable. It's the same with your children. How they feel about themselves will determine what happens outside of them. If they feel good about themselves, they will spend time on their hair, clothes, good grooming and good manners. As moms, it is our job to make sure that what's in them is right. Don't allow any negative talk to come out of them; instead always point them toward the positive.

~ I saw its value, treated it as valuable and it became valuable. ~

**Practical Ways To Encourage Your Kids**

The following are some practical things you can do that communicate love, acceptance, and encouragement to the hearts of your children.

Send a note in their lunch box. Even though you're all grown up now, wouldn't you give anything if you had just one note from your mother that said, "I'm proud of you, Daughter?" It takes thirty seconds of your time to write, but the memory and effects last a lifetime. Your children will open that note up at school, and they'll feel like they can take on the world. A note from Mom makes for a nice moment in the day.

Another thing you can do is write a letter to your child on birthdays and holidays. Your children get cards and letters from friends and relatives, and these cards are nice. But they shortly get tossed in the trash. The letters from mom, however, get placed in a special place—a special box or a folder in their closet. So on those days when they don't feel sure of themselves, when they feel life isn't going just right, they can pull those letters out and remind themselves of the security they have in Mom.

What would you give to have a letter from your mom pointing out all the things she was proud of in your life? How about a letter pointing out all the good in you? This would be truly something that even today would bring a smile to your face as you read it, and even on your worst days, that letter could make you feel good about yourself.

Another practical way to encourage your children is to plan to spend a few moments with them after a sporting event, dance recital, school play, spelling bee or a competition or activity of whatever kind. Point out the good things they did and make them feel special about their performance.

For one, this says to the child that Mom was watching; two, it says she cares; and, three, it helps get the good thoughts in before any bad thoughts have time to take root.

Look to the positive and then point them toward practice. And make sure you take time to work with them on what is important, like in the instance of my practicing piano with my son. I took twenty minutes a night and invested in my son's success. That is just a part of a TV show's worth of time that I invested in my son instead of just wasting it in front of a television.

Don't miss out on carving out even small amounts of meaningful time spent encouraging your kids. These few moments in the day that you invest will communicate to your child that what he's doing matters to Mom. Plus, nobody likes to stink at something. When you stink at something, it can tear down your self-image in more areas than just the event you're participating in at the moment. Don't allow your kid to be the one who can't catch or hit the ball. It took my husband only twenty minutes a day for a month for Laken to become very good at baseball. And the confidence that came from that month of practice showed up in many other areas of his life.

**The Power of Encouragement**
**To Heal a Broken Heart**

Make sure you are there in the times of disappointment in your kids' lives. Once again, your encouragement can head off wrong thoughts before they attach themselves to your children's self-esteem.

With each boy that broke my heart, or snotty girl at school who was rude and mean, my mom was right there. Every single time when I told her, she dropped what she was doing and would say, "Let's go get nachos," "Let's watch a movie," "Let's run to the mall." We would get to where we were going and she would just let me share and talk. And during this time, she would very smoothly direct me away from negatives about myself. Although after the shopping, I still hurt inside, I left with some hope and, as always, confidence in the love my mom had for me. To this day she is still doing this for me, but now it's, "Let's go to Starbucks!"

We should be our children's endless source of encouragement. With our words and our actions—cards, letters, thoughtful words and acts, and time spent together—we can be there to encourage them and to pick them up when they've fallen under the heavy weight of discouragement. We need to constantly be building their self-esteem so that they can become resilient to the pressures, criticisms and condemnation of the world.

Always see the good in your children and help them see the good themselves. Help them improve and overcome the weaknesses that they can change and finally, point them in the direction of success by instilling in them positive thoughts and beliefs about themselves. These thoughts and beliefs will fuel a winning self-image within them that will carry them into the great life you want for them.

# Chapter 15

## Give Me a Hug

Some things went wrong at home one day—terribly wrong. One of the air-conditioning units had stopped working, and we found out it was going to cost $1,200 to get it fixed. The garage door stopped working, and we couldn't get our cars out of the garage. When we finally got the garage door open manually, I got the car out but then was pulled over for speeding. The dog chewed up some toys that the kids weren't supposed to even take outside, much less leave them for the dog to get to. I was over budget, and Scot had mentioned it was "bill night." Our wood floor (the primary flooring throughout the house) was still not installed, making this the fourth month of cement floors. Workmen had had to punch holes in our basement walls looking for mold after the entire basement had been found flooded two days before. I was doing laundry and packing to leave early the next morning for our three-week vacation when I ran out of detergent. My oldest son had to be taken to the emergency room to have a gash stitched on his leg, which he sustained by cutting it on broken glass as he was dumping the trash. The icing on the cake was that nights' episode of, *Grey's Anatomy*, was a rerun.

In the midst of all this, my mom stopped over. As she pulled me out the door on a quest for coffee and Chai tea, she hugged me. I was thirty-five when this happened, yet I still cannot describe adequately what that hug meant to me. Is it enough to say that it meant everything? Although I was a grown woman, a mom myself, that hug from my mom seemed to diffuse the crisis and comforted raging and conflicting emotions. That hug lifted my spirits and empowered me. It said, "Tomorrow is another day; this too, shall pass."

In this short chapter, I'm going to talk about the power of healthy touch.

Moms must realize the power that resides in their arms. As a mom, your arms can bring love and encouragement to your children in any circumstance and at any age. They can bring comfort to a hurtful time. One of the greatest needs your children have is healthy touch.

Touch oftentimes says so much more than your words could ever convey. A pat on the back says, "I'm proud of you." A great big bear hug says, "Our relationship is fun." A grip on the shoulder says, "You can do it," and "I'm behind you." A hug in a time of pain says, "I am always there and everything is going to get better." A hug in a time of worry or anxiety says, "There's nothing to worry about when Mom is here." A great big exuberant hug says, "I missed you when you were gone," and, "You are an important part of my life that I can't live without." A rub on the shoulders conveys confidence and comfort.

With your arms, you can send messages all day that say to your children they can trust Mom, Mom is there for them, and she loves them.

When you hold your children, it meets special emotional needs. When that need is not met, children look to other places. If you don't hold your son, the wrong woman may. He will get that need met one way or another. If you don't hug your daughter, she will get that need met in other ways.

Do not deny your children this most basic human need. "But my kids don't like it. They push me away." That may be what they say on the outside, but on the inside, they're crying out for a touch from Mom. Your kids may push away and say, "Aw, come on, Mom." But you could say something like, "Mom needs a hug." (Of course, as you press on, don't be insensitive and embarrass them in front of their friends.) You're saying that you need it but really they need it. In a way, you have tricked them into allowing you to meet a need they have, yet they feel like they've met your need.

With your arms, you can send messages all day that say to your children they can trust Mom.

I say to my children, "Come on and sit by Mom during the TV show." I let them sit on my lap, or sometimes I wrestle with them. I know it's my job to make sure my children get the touch they need in their lives.

I wonder how many children are crying out to be held. Don't let a day go by without expressing love to your children through healthy touch.

I give my kids a huge hug when they leave for school. "Have a great day," and, "I will miss you. You are valuable to me." I give them a hug every time they get home from school.

I make sure that whenever my kids do something good, I give them verbal praise and then a squeeze on the shoulder or pat on the back. And watching a movie on TV with Mom is like one big dog pile. All four kids want me to hold them, and I let them sit on my lap. Finally, at night, I give them a big hug and a kiss goodnight. My kids get a minimum of three touches a day, but these touches will last a lifetime.

Understand that touch affects trust. Wrong touch in a relationship will immediately destroy the relationship. But right touch constantly builds trust. If you want to have a great relationship with your children, then appropriate touch has to be a part of that. I know it may seem like such a little thing, but if you add up all the little things you can do as a mother, the result will be success in the relationship.

You have great power to communicate how much you love your children, and that power is in your arms.

MOM

# Chapter 16

## I Will Be Going to School With You Today

This story is an account as told to me by one of my kids' favorite Sunday School teachers, Miss Penny. My two oldest children, Laken and Heath, are at the time six and five years old respectively. Both are being brought up in a good, godly home with parents who give their all to place God's values and His character into their little souls. To fully grasp the fun of this event, you must know that my husband is the associate pastor of his father's church of about 8,000 people. We teach the parenting class, from which more than 10,000 parents have graduated over the years. People watch me and my children closely to see if we live what we preach.

It is a beautiful Sunday morning. My two sons have just finished up their Bible time. Church is just getting out, and the children are playing with the toys as parents begin lining up at the door to pick up their blessings. Little children—children who are looking to my children for some guidance and direction—are playing all around the room. Miss Penny is talking to Heath on one side of the room, while Laken is on the other side playing with LEGOS.

Laken screams across the room, "Miss Penny, look at the ship I made!"

Heath's expression turns to immediate surprise, and he screams out, "Miss Penny, Laken just said SH@#!" (He said the actual word.)

He said it so loudly that Miss Penny and all the parents standing around clapped their hands over their mouths and said, "Oh, my gosh!"

In defense of himself, Laken screams back at Heath, "Nuh Uh! I didn't say SH@#—I said, ship!"

Heath screams back, "You did not! You said SH@#!"

Miss Penny is frantically trying to stop them. Laken screams again in front of all the parents and all those small, impressionable children, "I said ship, ship, ship—not SH@#!!!"

Heath, to the amazement of all, says in a calm, cool tone: "BULL SH@#!"

Here's an extreme example, but a great example. What would you do if a man came up and grabbed your three-year-old son from you? What would you do if some man came and snatched your four-year-old daughter out of your hands? Catch them and beat them within an inch of their life, right? When those words are spoken, anger rises up in you. A sense of protection rises up in you. You will lay down your life at that moment to protect your child. This is the attitude you must have for the rest of your life!

Take that same parent. Where does that instinct of protection go when she finds out her fifteen-year-old daughter is dating some twenty-three-year-old loser? "Well, we tried grounding her. Nothing seems work. So we just hope things turn out well."

Heck no! Just like that guy that tried to grab my three-year-old, I will still do whatever it takes, lay down my life to save hers! I will put bars on the windows, sleep in her room, go to school with her. I will spend every waking moment of my life guarding our little princess.

~ I will still do whatever it takes, lay down my life, to save hers! ~

Where is that instinct when the mother finds out her fourteen-year-old son is hanging out with the wrong crowd? "We tried to get him to stop hanging out with them. Nothing works." What works is your son has no friends. You become his only friend. You tell him, "If I have to, I will go to school with you, be in all your classes. We will have so much fun together. I am willing to lay down my life for you, even give up the love you have for me if that is what it takes."

At a time when many teenagers make decisions that ruin their lives or at least destroy a good part of it, my parents decided and made it clear, "No, we love you too much to allow you to do that." Too many parents don't take on the disciplinary role in the family. We want to be the good guy, the "good cop," the friend. Sure, friendship is our ultimate goal but if you step into that role too early, your child suffers, and in many cases will resent your lack of authority at a time in his life when he needed it most.

Sure, in the midst of consequence, your child will be mad and upset. But great parents don't care as much about the moment as they care about the end result.

When my husband, Scot, was in twelfth grade, the school was having trouble with him not attending classes. His dad found out and sat down with him to talk. I'm sure he had his cocky, "Okay, whatcha gonna do about it, Dad?" attitude running full throttle.

He said his dad responded, "Son, if you cut class one more time, I will have to take vacation from work. And then what I will do is go to school with you each day. Once again, I will be your best friend. We will sit in class together. I will go to lunch with you and hang out at the lockers with you. We will spend all day, every day together until I feel I can trust you to go to class."

Well, there was no way he was going to hang out with his Dad at school, so he didn't miss another class!

Your children have to know that you will do whatever it takes to help them make good choices in life.

I can't tell you how many times my husband and I have had parents meet with us, telling us they have no control over their teenage son or daughter. "My daughter sneaks out every night," one dad told us. Well, then our advice is that she will be sleeping in her parents' room every night until she stops sneaking out. "Well, she's fifteen and dating this guy, and I can't stop it." Yes, you can. You can do whatever it takes to protect your children from making life-destroying decisions.

**You Can Get Involved!**

Many parents sit back and say, "There's nothing we can do. We tried grounding him, but he sneaks out. We said 'No,' but he did it, anyway."

You have to ask yourself, what is your child's future worth? Up until the time your kids are out of the house, you are responsible for the decisions they make. Your fourteen-year-old daughter is dating a nineteen-year-old guy. That's your fault, and if you don't take care of it, your daughter will be setting her future up for disaster.

You have to have the mindset that you will do whatever it takes to change your kids' direction when they're headed down the wrong path. Wrong friends can destroy their lives, so until they show you that they can pick the right friends, it might be up to you to pick their friends. A wrong girlfriend can destroy your son's life. Obviously, if he can't pick the right girl, Mom and Dad will have to pick for him. If kids don't want to go to school, Mom and Dad can fix that. Mom and Dad will steer the kids' lives until they learn to steer them themselves. I'm not saying you should do this in an over-controlling way. Just don't let your kids walk down a destructive path. You have the power to stop them from hurting themselves.

Later in life, your child will say, as my husband did, "Thanks, Mom and Dad." When his parents did that for him, it built trust in him. His parents put up with his being mad and upset because they loved him enough to discipline him, loved him enough to say, "No." In that, respect and trust were built inside him.

You have to be your child's moral conscience until your child can make the right choices on his or her own. That means you make their decisions until they are at a point in life when they can make right decisions.

I have parents ask me all the time at what age a girl can date. I say, "How do I know? I don't know your daughter." There is no age at which all teenaged girls are ready to date. If she's seventeen years old, dating a drop-out loser with no job, and he treats her like garbage, guess what? She isn't old enough to date.

We had a father and mother one night show up at a meeting talking about how their fourteen-year-old daughter ran away the day before and how he and his wife decided that they wouldn't allow this to affect their lives. We told him, "You go get in the car, search the streets and go to the boyfriend's house and scare the living heck out of him."

"Yeah," her father said, "but she will just run away again."

I said, "That would be very hard to do with her father right by her side all the time. I tell you what, you go to school with her and to class with her. You have lunch together. You wait outside the stall in the women's bathroom if you have to. Let her know that you love her so much, you will lay down your life so she doesn't end up losing hers."

Moms have said, "But I can't get her to stop dating this bum." I guarantee I could! "I can't get my son to go to school." I guarantee I could! "I can't get my son to hang out with the right friends." I guarantee I could! Why am I so confident? Because I know that I would lay my life down so that my children wouldn't lose theirs. But many moms today give up their children's future because they give up on the moment. They have this attitude of just giving up and leaving their kids' futures to whatever happens.

His parents put up with his being mad and upset because they loved him enough to discipline him, loved him enough to say, "No."

You have to be able to say, "Can't pick out right music? Guess what—I will pick it." "Can't be responsible with how much TV you watch? Guess what—I will show you how." "Failing your classes? Guess what—I will call the teacher every day, get the assignment for the night, and sit beside you while you do your homework. We will check it and go over it until it is perfect. I will know when your tests are, and I will teach you how to study. And until you can get good grades on your own, Mom will be right there to make sure you do."

Until your children have the mental capacity to make right choices, it is your responsibility to make the choices for them—end of story.

That is the heart and attitude of a great mom. Anything less, and the rest of this book can be used to clean up the dog's mess. You see, all kids test the water, but if Mom isn't willing to dive in to save her son or daughter from drowning, does anything else she's accomplished really matter?

Your children may hate it at the time, but if you don't discipline them, down the road they may resent you for allowing them to ruin their lives!

**Learn How To Discipline Rightly**

I feel it's important that you learn how to properly discipline in love. This book is not about that, so go out and get other books that specifically deal with discipline. Find out the right ways to discipline in love.

For you to read this chapter and then just start spanking your kids is not my intention, and it will do more damage than good. I believe that to randomly spank or discipline without any training is more damaging than not disciplining at all. It's like throwing an eight-year-old behind the wheel of a car and saying, "Drive!" He will do more damage than good.

You can't just go into the programming files of your computer and type in random things. You will mess it up. You have to learn the codes, when to do things and when not to. It's the same thing with your kids. There are plenty of books, tapes and other material on raising kids. Get hold of some of them and learn how to discipline correctly.

This knowledge will give you confidence. You see, when I know that what I'm doing is right, I can step out into disciplining my children more confidently. But if I'm not sure—if I think, Maybe it is right, maybe it's not—it keeps me from stepping out. Or I try something half way, it didn't really work, so I give up. Now I try something else.

Most of the time, it doesn't work because you're not committed to it. Kids are smart. They know they just have to wait out the new discipline fad. If I pout long enough, throw a big enough fit, my parents will give up. Why do they give up? Because they lack confidence in it. Many parents do nothing because they have no confidence. And who ends up suffering? The child whose parents gave him no direction or structure.

Kids who have direction, structure and discipline in their lives are a lot happier than kids who do not. How would you like to work at a job where you never knew what was expected of you? Some days you got in trouble for one thing, but the next day, you didn't get in trouble for something you did that was even worse. And then some days, if the boss was moody, you got in trouble for nothing at all. It would be a very confusing, annoying world.

Kids are the same; they are happier when they know what to expect. Kids whose parents go off on them on every whim of emotion—sometimes they get in trouble for this; at other times, they don't—experience a very confusing world. The real problem with this is that kids are gamblers at heart. They think that if they get into trouble only one out of three times for something, more than likely, they will try it again.

I said all that to say this: Learn how to discipline your kids with consistency. Get into some classes and get some books if you need to. But stay the course! A great proverb says, "Train up a child in the way he should go, and when he is old he will not depart from it." You see, it is your job to train them up through proper, consistent discipline.

In all this, remember that the goal of discipline is to change direction. If my child is headed down a wrong road, how do I change his or her direction? Each child is a little different. For some kids, taking away the phone and TV will change their direction. Others may need a more strict approach.

Kids who have direction, structure and discipline in their lives are a lot happier than kids who do not.

MOM

# Chapter 17

## I Love You! Now Leave Me Alone

Another great story told from Scot's perspective: "Little Peyton is my two-year-old and is quite possibly the cutest thing in the world. He has blonde, super curly hair and a smile that can melt your heart. If you were to ask me Peyton's favorite place in the world, I wouldn't say Disneyland, LEGOLAND, or even the beach. I would have to say it is our pantry. To Peyton, this enormous place filled with cookies, toaster pastries, cereal bars, chips, candy and other goodies, is heaven. We have a huge walk-in pantry with a glass door that we have to keep closed or Peyton would weigh 400 pounds. But in the course of any given day, somebody leaves the door open, and into heaven Peyton will go.

"You can always tell when Peyton has entered the pantry, because, all of a sudden, you'll hear him scream out, 'YEAHHH!!!' as he claps his hands. He does realize that after his scream of excitement, he has only about fifteen seconds to eat all he can.

"So here we are, just before time to leave for church. Holly is already at the church teaching, which leaves me alone with the children. I'm in the middle of combing my four year-old's hair when I hear, 'YEAHHH!!!'

"I stop what I'm doing and go to the pantry. To my surprise, Peyton is scaling the shelves like a skilled mountain climber. He already has in his hands the candy tote and is lowering it to the floor.

"I say, 'Peyton, no.'

"He says, 'Daddy, nanny.' He then looks at me with those huge blue eyes and says, 'Pleeeeeze? Just on' (that's one), Daddy?'

"I say, 'Okay, just one.'

"I give him one little candy, close the pantry, and go back to combing Baylor's hair.

"Not two minutes later, I hear, 'YEAHHH!!!'

"What in the world…, I think, as I rush over the pantry again. Now Peyton is shoveling candy into his mouth. He says, 'Mmm, Daddy, mmm.'

"'No, Peyton. No more candy!'

"He then swallows the pound of candy and points his tiny finger at me and says, 'No, Daddy, no! On' more nanny!'

"I say, 'No,' and I take the candy tote away from him and remove him from the pantry.

"In an instant, Peyton goes from happy little son to screaming son. Now, we don't allow fits in my house, so I put him in the corner, which is really cute to see him cry in the corner while we laugh at him (that last part about laughing is a joke, but it is cute).

"Once again, I try to finish combing Baylor's hair when all of a sudden, I hear the tap, tap, tap of little feet running. Peyton is making a break for the pantry. In amazement, I'm thinking, Do you really think I can't catch you? I put the comb down and start to walk over to the pantry when Peyton closes the door. I'm thinking, What! Do you really think I can't open that door? But then he locks the door from the inside!

"I now have my face pressed up against the glass, watching him clap his hands and scream, 'YEAHHH!!!'

"I scream out, 'Peyton, you open this door!'

"He stops clapping, looks at me, and says, 'No, Da-Da, no!' He then opens the candy tote and begins to eat.

"I say, 'No, Peyton!'

"He looks at me and says, 'Yes, yes!'

"I scream out, 'PEYTON, YOU OPEN THIS DOOR RIGHT NOW! PUT THAT CANDY DOWN RIGHT NOW! DO YOU HEAR ME?'

"To my great amazement, he turns to me, puts his finger to his lips, and goes, 'Sshhhhh.' (That was funny.)

"I scream, 'Someone get Daddy a screwdriver—Dad's breaking into the pantry!'

To my great amazement, he turns to me, puts his finger to his lips, and goes, "Sshhhhh."

"I run to the garage, get a screwdriver, come back in, and begin to pick the lock. Peyton, understanding what is happening, begins to shove all the candy he possibly can into his mouth. He's probably figuring, If I'm going to get a spanking, I will make sure it's worth it."

As you read this chapter, realize that I saved some of the most important things for last. The material contained in this chapter has to do with setting the mood in your home, and I'll just say this. The mood you consistently set in your home will affect, for good or bad, the relationship you will have with your children when they are grown.

Picture the following scenario. Here you are out to lunch with an acquaintance or friend. This made-up scenario is one I would be willing to bet we've all had happen with our kids at home. All of a sudden, in the middle of the meal, your adult friend knocks over a glass of milk that she was drinking.

Now, how do you respond to this person who probably won't be in your life in a few years—this person who doesn't mean half as much to you as your own child? Do you say, "What in the world are you doing? Where is your head? Can you not focus for two minutes? Can't you use two hands on your glass like you're supposed to? Will you look at that—it's all over the place!" (It's funny how we always want our kids to look at it.) "What am I supposed to do?" your rampage continues. "Now I have to clean up your mess, because you can't watch what you're doing! You know what—you're never going to get milk in a glass ever again. From now on, we're just going to put all your drinks in a sippy cup."

Is that how you would respond to your friend or acquaintance—this relatively meaningless person in your life? Probably not. But how do you respond to your child in similar situations? Do you give him or her the same type of respect as this person who in ten years probably won't remember you?

How about a scenario in which you're working at your office, you're busy, and a co-worker comes up to you and says, "Hey, I have a quick question for you." How do you respond to this co-worker whom you barely even know?

Do you say, "Can I not have two or three minutes to myself? I just want to get some things done around here! Can life not be about you all day? Can I have a little peace and quiet for one minute! I'd like to have just three minutes at a time when I could just focus on something I want to focus on. You know what—go to your cubicle and don't you come out till I get done!"

Is that how you would respond to your co-worker? No, of course it isn't. But do you show your children at least the same emotional stability that you would show a person who means nothing to you? Could your children have that much from you?

Now listen to my heart on this. I'm not saying that we're to be our kids' best friends who can never meet out any kind of discipline or a reprimand when it's called for. No, I'm still the parent. I'm still guiding and directing my children, and, hopefully, by the age of nineteen, my goal of friendship will be attained. However, how I, as a mother, respond to my children should always be about relationship building, not about emotional rampaging that tears the relationship down.

**The Relationship Should Affect the Response**

If you went off like I described earlier on your friend who spilled her milk, would you have any chance at a friendship with her? Probably not. For the same reason you wouldn't berate your friend, you should also change your responses to your kids. If one of my kids is fooling around and spills a glass of milk, I remain calm because I don't want to do anything to hinder the relationship. I reply, "You know what—when you have milk in a glass, you need to watch what you're doing. I want you right now to clean up the milk. And if you can't handle the responsibility of milk in a glass, Mom's going to have to give you a sippy cup until you can."

If I want a relationship with my child, I will just calmly deal with the situation. I won't scream, holler and yell. I won't look like a lunatic or a nut in front of my child, going off because of a little bit of spilled milk in his life. Most importantly, I won't hurt the relationship over something as meaningless as milk.

If your children keep interrupting you while you work, teach them how to do it correctly. If you teach your children how to interrupt correctly, when they become adults, interrupting other adults will not be annoying to all those around them.

So I taught my kids how to interrupt, and when they do come to talk to me while I'm busy, first, I take a breath and think to myself, My children's needs are very important to me. Then I reply, "Is this an emergency? No? Okay, Mom's in the middle of doing something right now. If you'll give me about twenty or thirty minutes, Mom's going to come help you, and she's going to take care of your problem."

~ Do you see the difference in the response when relationship is important? ~

Do you see the difference in the response when relationship is important? I've done it the other way when I've been busy with something frustrating. One of my children would come to me with a question and out of me would come garbage. I had to change, and you may need to change, too.

This chapter is about changing probably the most important area of our lives. If you will change this one area, I believe you will change everything. Again, I'm talking about setting the mood of your home.

**The Mood of the Home Mirrors the Mother**

When my husband told me that he was going to write that Dad is one who sets the atmosphere or mood of the home, I said that, no, Mom is the one who sets the mood of the home. This discussion led to a fight, during which he really made me mad, and I proved to him that I have the power to set the mood of the home!

What emotion you bring to breakfast seems to linger and follow the kids throughout the day. What you bring home sets the atmosphere for the night.

If Mom is happy and excited about the day in the morning and comes home happy and excited about the night, soon the family will be excited about life, too. If Mom is moody and nobody can talk to her in the morning, or if they have to leave mom alone when she gets home, that home can become a heavy, dark, and uninviting place.

What most moms don't realize is that what they set up in the home is what their kids take into the world and into their future homes. The atmosphere you reflect can dictate how they see the world, life and relationships.

**Put on a Smile and Make Happiness a Choice**

I almost didn't think to talk in this book about what Mom reflects in the home, because moodiness wasn't allowed in my home growing up. As a habit, my mom was not down, depressed or moody. Now, she had plenty of circumstances and excuses to be, yet she wasn't. When my mom was working almost 100 hours a week, for little to no pay, taking care of fourteen juvenile boys, that would have been a reasonable excuse to be tired, irritable and moody. But she wasn't.

When my dad got laid off for a year, and my mom had to go to work, that could have been a perfect excuse for her to be depressed and think, Poor me! Life isn't fair, and I think I'm going to have a mid-life crisis. But she didn't. No matter what happened in life, my mom demonstrated that happiness is a choice.

We will always have problems in life, but how you deal with them dictates how successful and great your life will be. I now carry over into my life the heritage my mother gave me. Every day of life is great! I have an amazing, happy, joy-filled life. Though I have big problems just like everyone else, I know that problems don't have to dictate my mood and that other people can't make me feel something; I dictate my mood.

I hear of homes in which the family knows not to talk to Mom in the morning. She just isn't a morning person (she doesn't love others until after lunch). Then when Mom gets home, the family knows to leave her alone until after dinner. And the kids walk around on eggshells, so to speak, because Mom is stuck in her depression and might go off at any time.

**Whose Image Are You Reflecting?**

As a mom, it is your job to guide and direct the entire family in the direction of having a home that is full of love, joy, peace and kindness.

A home environment as intended, is one in which something is different when someone steps into your home. Yours is a home where happiness reigns in the home. If one of your children's friends comes over any time of any day, he should be able to say to you, "Something's different about this house. How come this house is so different? How come this house is so happy? How come when you ask your kids to do something, they do it without throwing a fit and slamming doors? What is different about this house?"

It is your responsibility as a mother to get up every day with the attitude, This is a great day! Circumstances will not direct my day. Instead, I direct my day. I show my day how I'm supposed to feel. And as I begin to interact with my kids, I teach them, too, that circumstances don't dictate or direct our emotions.

It is interesting that in life, you almost always get what you expect. If you expect a bad day, you get a bad day. But if you expect a great day, you almost always get a great day. In my life, I have never had a bad day. Sure I had some negative circumstances, but at the end of the day, all the greatness in my life outweighs the bad. If at the end of the day I have my handsome husband and four boys, what else do I need?

Every day you should get up and expect a great day. This is what you should demonstrate to your children. Moodiness and crabbiness should not be allowed in your home. Teach your children to put a smile on their faces when they come to breakfast. The rule should be, "If you're not happy, then go back to your room. When you can be happy, come on out, because we are one happy family!"

It is your responsibility as a mother to get up every day with the attitude, This is a great day!

I was running errands one day, and I knew I was going to be doing a lot of in and out of the car, so I really should have just left the kids with a sitter. I was on a deadline, and my mind was very full and my thoughts were running every which way. To put it mildly, I had allowed myself to become quite stressed.

We were nearing the end of our trip out and about when my two youngest started arguing with each other.

"No, I didn't."

"Yes, you did."

"No, I didn't."

"Yes, I saw you. You did,"

"Nu uhh!"

"Yes huh!"

On and on and on. All I remember is inhaling, then, "Shut up! Shut up! Just Shut Up! Got it? Just

CLOSE your Mouth! Shut UP! Shut it! Say nothing! BE QUIET!"

Silence. Then, from the very back of my vehicle, my six-year-old, Baylor, says, "Wow, doesn't SOMEONE need to capture HER thoughts!"

In the mornings growing up, I might not have had a good night. My day might not have been all it should or could be. But when you came out to breakfast at the Adam's house, you put on a smile like Mom's. You said good morning and acted happy. Funny thing is, no matter how I felt when I got up, by the time breakfast was over, I honestly could say, "This is going to be a great day."

It is a mother's job to train her children in the direction of a happy home atmosphere. She is to train her children not to be moody. "We're not cranky in this home; we don't do those things. This home isn't moody, isn't depressed. This home is up and happy." Moms, make sure Dad follows the rules, too. "Sorry, Dad, go back to your room until you can come down happy. Sorry, Dad, we don't get to be moody after work. You will need to figure out how to get yourself happy."

Mom is to train her children and demonstrate to them what the correct attitude of the home should be. And as she begins to change the attitude of the home, she begins to change the attitude her kids will take out into the world. They will no longer take the moodiness and other junk with them out into the world. Instead, they are a bright light of great emotions that shines forth into the lives of others.

It is Mom and Dad's responsibility to set the mood of happiness in this home every day. How sad is it for a child to learn before he goes off to school that he can't talk to his dad or mom? His dad's in the newspaper or busy watching ESPN in the morning. Mom is on the phone. The child then goes off into the world thinking maybe the world will answer some of his questions—maybe the world will be there for him. The child will hope that the world can give him some sort of security, because he can't get it at home.

You know, when Dad gets home from work, his children have missed him all day but how often do they know to keep away from him because he's going to be cranky from the stress of work and the traffic coming home? He has to go off by himself and watch TV for a few hours while the rest of the family keeps quiet. How sad is it that kids can't get excited about seeing Dad come home and being able to share their day with him and have him share his with them? Moms, tell Dad to get happy!!!

**At Your House, Is It All About You?**

When kids have to walk around the house on egg-shells because Mom's deep in depression, something is wrong in that house. Everything has to be quiet and perfect or Mom will go off on them. All of sudden, the kids are trying to figure out how they can fix Mom's world, how they can make Mom happy. And so they're doing this, that and the other thing, trying to make Mom happy.

Kids have enough to worry about without worrying about fixing your life. They should be focused on getting their lives in order!

There are moms out there who will steal their kid's money to buy booze and drugs. These moms will sell their kid's PlayStations® or Xboxes™ to get drugs. As horrible as that sounds, do you want to know what I feel is worse? A parent who steals her child's joy. I really do feel it's worse. It takes a very self-centered person to steal their kid's PlayStation® or bike. We probably all could agree on that. But what kind of person would steal their child's joy and happiness?

"Well, you don't understand. I'm depressed," you might say. So that gives you a right to steal your kid's joy? That's the same excuse the drug addict uses, "Well you don't understand. I need the drugs!"

Depression is oftentimes simply about self. Now, obviously, some depression is clinical and requires medical attention, but I'm talking about the selfish kind of depression that is consumed with "my past, my circumstances, my stress, my anxieties, my heartache, my pain, my life!" Furthermore, these people have the attitude that says, Because of how I feel, I will make everyone around me feel miserable. I have no joy and happiness, so I will steal theirs. I have my moodiness, my stress on the job and my things to worry about. Therefore, I will put all of these things on my children and rob them of their joy and happiness in their home life. That is my right.

But you never, ever have the right to steal a child's happiness, to take away his joy or peace. You never have a right to exalt your problems and emotions as more important than anyone else's, as if to say, "My problems and emotions are more important than yours. So I will pull you down and make you feel bad because I feel bad. What you're feeling doesn't matter. What matters is how I feel."

~ Kids have enough to worry about without worrying about fixing your life. ~

### The Memory Kids Take With Them Will Determine the Relationship You'll Have With Them

I'm not saying that, as moms, we are never to make a single mistake. Remember, it's how we're characterized overall that counts. I know in my own life, there will still be a day now and then when I'm feeling a little stressed. I'm still going to have days when things didn't go well. Growing up, my mom may have had a bad day or two—but, you see, I can't remember them, because my mom was characterized as being a great mom every day. She was characterized in my childhood as being happy. And so in my lifetime, all I can remember is that my house—my home life—was happy. As I said, moodiness was never a part of my home. We were not allowed to be moody and unhappy at our house.

**Let's Not Kill Heath Today!**

Scot and Baylor were sitting at the table coloring, having "Dad and Baylor Time." Laken had a friend over, and it was about eight o'clock at night. They had asked if they could go outside to eat their popsicles, when all of a sudden, they come running in the door.

Slam! Laken and his friend have this exaggerated expression of fake terror, and they have their hands across the door as if they're going to protect us from impending danger. Laken's friend cries out, "He's trying to kill us!"

Now, Laken and his friend were playing a little pretend game of "the bad guy is outside trying to get us." I know this, you know this, Scot knows this, but Baylor doesn't know this.

Laken's friend says again, "He's trying to kill us right now."

Scot says, "Boys, we don't talk like that." Then, as if to play along with them somewhat, he says, "All right, guys, go downstairs and play, and everything will be fine."

So they go downstairs and we don't think anything more about it. Baylor and Scot continue coloring, and Heath comes into the kitchen. Understand that although Heath and Baylor are very good friends, Heath tends to tease Baylor a little bit—actually, quite a bit. Heath comes over and is peeking over Baylor's shoulders, grabbing his crayons and just being annoying.

I say, "Heath, we don't do mean things to our brother. I need you to go find something to do. Dad is having 'Dad and Baylor Time' right now."

Heath says, "Mom, can I go outside and get my truck?"

"Yes, Son."

Just as Heath was about to open the door, Baylor looks up, and Scot and I can see the fear on his face. He cries out, "HEATH, YOU CAN'T GO OUTSIDE! THERE'S A…" (long pause as he thinks for a minute). Then Baylor says, "Never mind" and goes back to his coloring.

**Outside Stimuli That Affects the Atmosphere of the Home**

You see, as a mom, doing the things that maintain peace in your home is your responsibility. What your kids see in you, they will do. You need to understand that what is going into your kids will come out of them and will affect their lives. What I allow to be poured into the minds of my children, whether it's through TV, radio, or anything else, will come out of them into every area of their lives.

I adapted this last point from Zig Ziglar's *How to Raise Positive Kids in a Negative World*[3], one of the best books I've read on this subject.

To understand the importance of monitoring the outside stimuli and influences that knock on the doors of your kids' minds, you will need to answer the following question. Suppose I was to gather all of your youth in one auditorium and then stand up before them and say, "Young adults, I'm here to tell you that getting drunk is awesome. Drugs are awesome. You're a nobody if you don't do drugs. To be popular, you need to try some drugs. And you need to have all the sex you can. And get into bestiality and the worship of idols. Murder is definitely something you have to try. And hate your parents. Don't listen to them—they're fools. Now go out and do all of these things. These are great, amazing experiences—please try them." (And then imagine that I added a little rhythm and used some poetic four-letter words.)

More than ninety-nine percent of parents, including those who aren't Christians, would be in an uproar. The news media would be all over it, and everyone would wish me ill. I guarantee I would no longer be allowed to speak to or further "motivate" your children. You would be so mad and upset.

Yet so many parents, including Christians, have no problem at all with the music they listen to or the TV and movies they watch. Most parents would be shocked to find out that everything I just said about drugs, sex and murder is being said to their kids every day, all day long, through music and TV. Most parents have no clue as to what is going into their kids' minds. Then they are genuinely confused by what is coming out of their kids—their kids' words and their behavior. The parents don't understand the rebellion, hate and anger that begin to show up in their own home.

~ Most parents have no clue as to what is going into their kids' minds. ~

Understand, I am not saying young people shouldn't be allowed to listen to anything but Christian music because there is a lot of good music out there. But I am saying that there is some heavy, hard stuff out there that your kids should not be allowed to listen to. And you can recognize most of it by just looking at the album covers. For example, if you pick up a CD and on the cover are three girls with everything "popping out" all over the place, you can know that these are probably not the people you want speaking into your daughter's life.

Studies have been conducted that show that kids who listen to heavy rock-and-roll music that has bestiality and other illicitness in it are 1,000 percent more likely to rebel against their parents, use drugs, and even commit suicide.

"Well, they're sixteen years old, and I can't control what they listen to." Yes, you can. You are in charge of their moral conscience until they can make the right choice.

In my own life, I was not able to pick out my own music until my parents felt like I could pick out the right music. That's just how it worked. So it was not until tenth grade that my parents finally said, "We now believe that you can take on the responsibility of choosing the right music. But if you go to the wrong music, we'll take that responsibility away."

I said in a previous chapter that your kids shouldn't get to choose until they choose right. In other words, just because your daughter is sixteen doesn't mean she's ready to choose the right music; she may not be mature enough to handle it.

I challenge you to tell your kids, "Mom's going to take your CD today and listen to it. I'm going to get hip today. I'm going to listen to it, and I'm going to find out what's going on in your head because it is very important to me. I will make sure I guard your emotions until you learn to guard them yourself."

I've talked to so many parents who felt like they were doing a good job parenting but were confused because their house was full of rebellion. Their kids were angry and depressed. They hadn't monitored what was going into them—that stimuli from without that has the potential to destroy their kids' lives.

I talked a lot about watching the type of music your kids listen to but, really, the same goes for TV. What are you allowing to come into your living room and into your family's lives?

I encourage you to keep track of just how much TV is going into your kids this week. You will be very surprised, like I was, to find that they could be watching five or more hours a day. And all the while they're watching TV, they're not using their imagination, building their problem-solving skills, strengthening their IQ, developing their relationship skills, or getting the physical exercise they need to live healthy, balanced lives in every area. They're just sitting, zoned out, with no memories being built inside them.

As a Mom, you are responsible for setting the mood of the home, for guarding the emotions of the home and for always pointing the home to the love, joy, peace and happiness that we should have. When these characteristics are in your heart as a mother, you can effectively guide your children into bright and beautiful futures with happy memories of home and an ongoing relationship with Mom that they will carry into the lives of their own children.

As we finish this journey of ours, I encourage you to go back and reread this book. Statistically, you only remember about twenty percent of what you read the first time. Having read this manuscript many times as the author, I have found myself growing and changing a little bit each time I read it. As I read about the importance of communication, for example, I think, I have forgotten lately to be sensitive to my family's needs in that area. Then I'll think, I need to reevaluate my values and priorities. I need to spend some more quality time with my husband. I need to plan for more family time, creating lifetime memories.

I also remember I need to be sensitive to my children's secret place, their inner world, as they share places in their hearts with me that are vulnerable and sacred. I don't want to miss that "window."

As I read further along, I allow these important principles to sink more deeply into my heart and mind. I am reminded of the need to continue to set the right mood in my home. My husband would laugh, because often when he entered my office, my eyes would be welled up with tears, and I'd say, "Boy, this is good. It just changed my life all over again."

So as strange as it sounds, each time I read this book, it helps me grow and keep changing. It reminds me that I have committed to being the most awesome mom within my ability. It helps me get back on track as I fulfill my vision for great mothering. It reminds me of what I am responsible for and to whom I'm responsible. Every one of us gets busy in life with things we need to do. If we don't remind ourselves of the things that are important, we can slip into neglecting the things that really matter in life.

I challenge you to never stop growing and changing. Get that vision inside you, in your heart and mind, for developing a great relationship with your children. Then keep that vision going so that at the end of your life, your children will be able to say about you, "There lies my best friend, my hero, my mom."

[3]Ziglar, Zig, *How to Raise Positive Kids in a Negative World.* New York : Ballantine Books, a division of Random House, Inc., 1989.

If we don't remind ourselves of the things that are important, we can slip into neglecting the things that really matteer in life.

MOM

## Featured Products by Winword Authors:

Scot Anderson
Dr. C. Thomas Anderson
Maureen Anderson
Jason Anderson

*Think Like a Billionaire, Become a Billionaire*

*Who's the Boss?*

*What in Health do You Want?*

*Finding Solitude With God*

*Wisdom Wins 1*

*Wisdom Wins 2*

*Confessing God's Word*

*Damaged DNA*

*Me, My Country, My God*

To order or for more information,
visit Winword Publishing House online at:

www.winwordpublishing.com

Or contact us at:
480-985-6156
or
www.DadMomBook.com

Winword
publishing house